Level 2 Diploma for IT Users
for City & Guilds

Website Design

for Office XP

Level
2

K Mary Reid

Endorsed by
**City&
Guilds**

Heinemann
Inspiring generations

Heinemann Educational Publishers
Halley Court, Jordan Hill, Oxford OX2 8EJ
Part of Harcourt Education

Heinemann is the registered trademark of
Harcourt Education Limited

Text © K Mary Reid 2004

First published 2005

07 06 05 04
10 9 8 7 6 5 4 3 2 1

British Library Cataloguing in Publication Data is available
from the British Library on request.

ISBN 0 435 46256 3

Publisher's note
The materials in this Work have been developed by Harcourt Education and the
content and the accuracy are the sole responsibility of Harcourt Education. The City
and Guilds of London Institute accepts no liability howsoever in respect of any
breach of the intellectual property rights of any third party howsoever occasioned or
damage to the third party's property or person as a result of the use of this Work.

The City & Guilds name and logo are the registered trademarks of the City and
Guilds of London Institute and are used under licence.

Typeset by Tech-Set Ltd, Gateshead, Tyne & Wear
Printed in UK by Thomson Litho

Acknowledgements
The screenshots in this book are reproduced with permission from Microsoft
Corporation.

The Disney logo and trademark are property of Disney Enterprise Inc., and are
reproduced by kind permission.

Tel: 01865 888058 www.heinemann.co.uk

Contents

Introduction

City & Guilds e-Quals is an exciting new range of IT qualifications developed with leading industry experts. These comprehensive, progressive awards cover everything from getting to grips with basic IT to gaining the latest professional qualifications.

The range consists of both user and practitioner qualifications. User qualifications (Levels 1–3) are ideal for those who use IT as part of their job or in life generally, while practitioner qualifications (Levels 2–3) have been developed for those who need to boost their professional skills in, for example, networking or software development.

e-Quals boasts online testing and a dedicated website with news, support materials and web-based training. The qualifications reflect industry standards and meet the requirements of the National Qualifications Framework.

With e-Quals you will not only develop your expertise, you will gain a qualification that is recognised by employers all over the world.

This unit is about designing and creating websites. It assumes that you have a basic level of IT skill and have spent some time exploring and using websites. You will learn to analyse the sites that you visit, and to use this experience when you come to design your own.

Creating a website is a challenging task, and is not nearly as straightforward as word processing a document. You have to think carefully about the purpose of the site and the kinds of people who will use it. Many aspects of design must be considered – the visual appearance, the way in which the pages are linked, the layout of the pages and the type of image formats that are suitable.

In addition you have to bear in mind the fact that each visitor to your site can set up their system to suit their own needs, so your pages may be viewed on a variety of browsers, in different sized windows, at different resolutions and with different default text and colour settings – and yet each page must be effective in all circumstances. Technical issues also have to be remembered, such as time taken to download a page and its images, and the fonts that may be installed on the visitor's system.

You will face, and solve, all these problems as the book takes you step by step through the design and creation of a number of websites. By the end you should be confident enough in your own skills to create a website, perhaps for a community group or for a small business.

Although the book covers the syllabus for City and Guilds IT User Level 2 Diploma Unit 208, it would also be useful for anyone who wants to learn how to create a straightforward website.

The City & Guilds syllabus does not prescribe the software that you should use. However, the terminology used and the skills included in the syllabus do point towards using Microsoft FrontPage. With this in mind each task that follows specifically refers to FrontPage.

Note on screenshots
The screenshots in this book show the 2002 version of FrontPage run on the Windows XP operating system in Classic mode. The same windows on your computer might look slightly different, however, the content and menus will be the same as long as your system is running Windows XP.

The basics

You will learn to

- Describe the effects that different screen resolutions and colour depths have on web pages
- Explain the significance of the speed of the Internet connection between the user's computer and the Internet (different file sizes and download times)
- Describe the main features and capabilities found in web browsers
- View the Hypertext Markup Language (HTML) for a web page
- Describe the importance of the pixel
- Recognise the different graphics file formats suitable for use in a web page
- Explain the issues involving copyright relevant to Internet websites

This section starts off by providing you with some basic information about websites. Without this, some aspects of web design will seem very puzzling indeed. It is easy to assume that the process of designing and creating a website is very similar to desktop publishing, but you will discover that there are many important differences between the two.

In particular, you need to be aware of:

- The technical issues and limitations in creating a website.
- The constraints imposed by the screens and settings that website visitors use.
- The variations in browsers.

Viewing web pages

Web browsers

A browser is a piece of software used to view pages on the World Wide Web. The most commonly used browser is Microsoft Internet Explorer, but other browsers, such as Netscape, are also used.

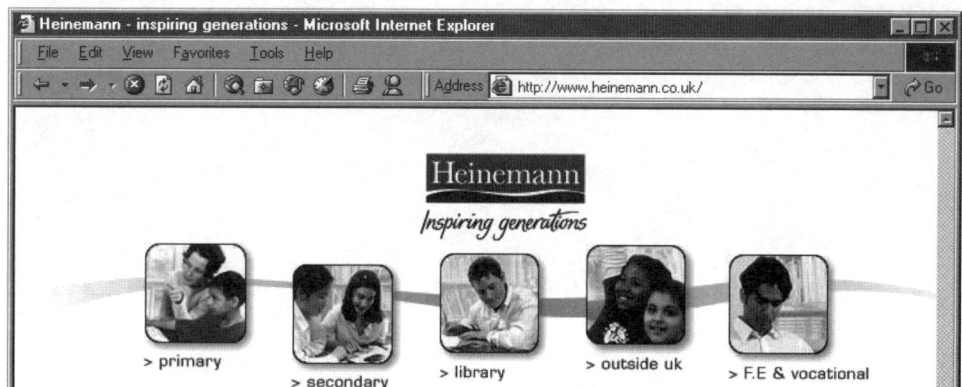

Figure 1.1 The Internet Explorer web browser

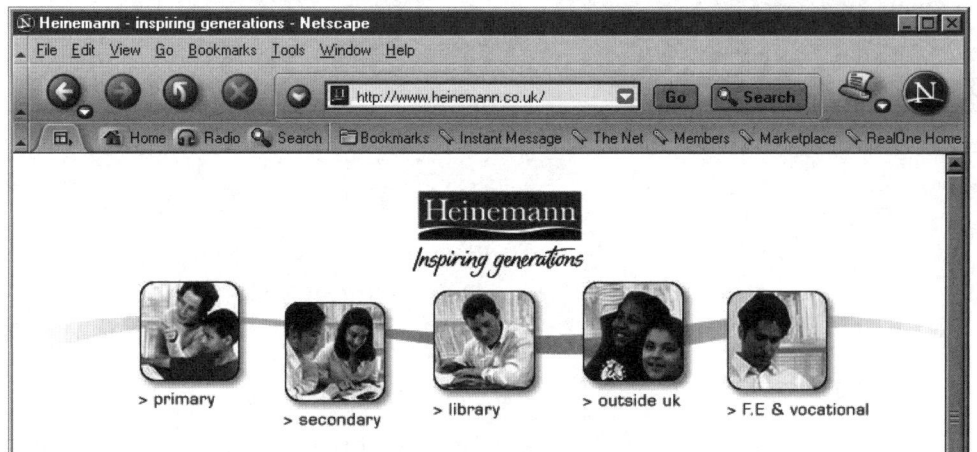

Figure 1.2 The Netscape web browser

A web browser uses a window to display a web page. The browser window can fill the screen or it can be reduced in size by the user. The amount that can be displayed within a window depends on the screen resolution.

Screen resolutions

A screen displays many dots of colour, known as pixels (derived from 'picture cells'). The number of pixels that can be displayed, width × height, is known as the screen resolution. For any one screen it is usually possible to change the screen resolution, although there will be a maximum resolution for each screen.

Task 1.1	Identifying and changing the screen resolution

Method

1   Select **Settings** and **Control Panel** in the **Start** menu.
2   Select **Display**, and in the dialogue box, click on the **Settings** tab (Figure 1.3).
3   Note the screen resolution you are using (given under the Screen area slider).
4   Use the Screen area slider to change the screen resolution. As you move the slider you will see the resolutions that your screen can support.

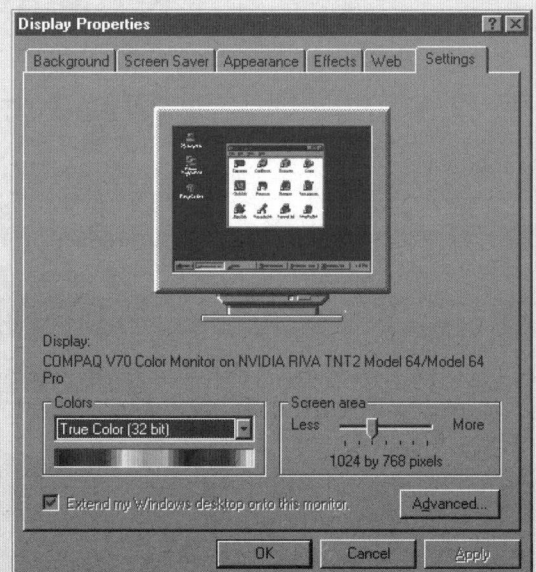

Figure 1.3 The Display Properties dialogue box

Information

Typical resolutions are 1280×960 (high resolution), 1024×768, 800×600 and 640×480 (low resolution). Note that they all maintain the ratio of $4:3$. The 640 pixel width is rarely used these days.

Your choice of screen resolution will depend on the physical dimensions of the screen. For example, it is difficult to read text on a small screen set at high resolution. This is particularly significant for small laptop screens. A user with visual impairment might also choose a lower screen resolution to give enlarged images and text.

Window sizes

The user can always change the size of a browser window, and it does not have to fill the whole screen. When a screen is set comfortably at a high resolution, many viewers take advantage of the extra space to display several windows at the same time. So they may well keep the browser window at a smaller size within the overall screen.

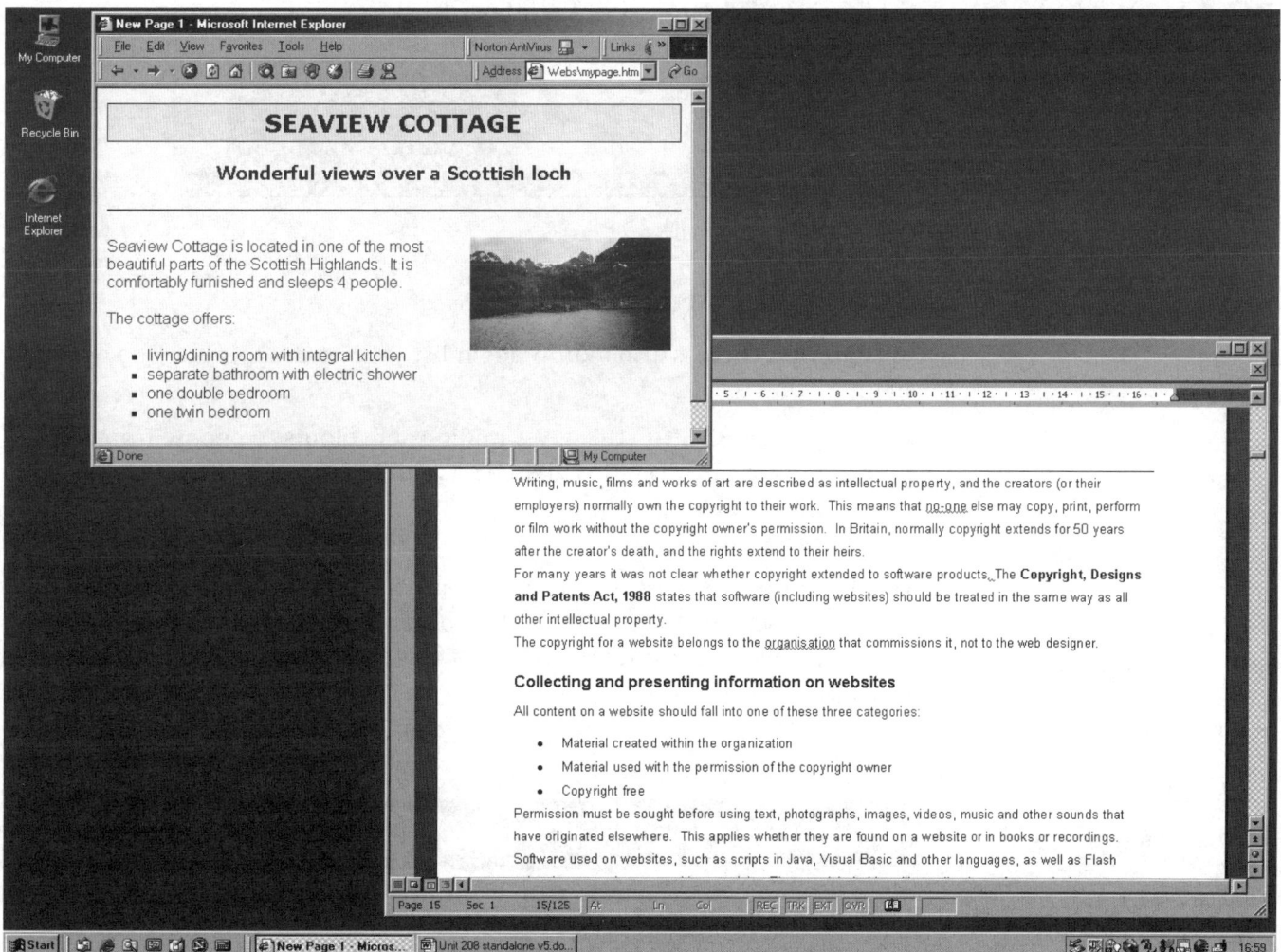

Figure 1.4 High resolution setting which uses a smaller browser window

This means that even when used on a high resolution setting, the actual display area of a web page cannot be determined with any degree of certainty.

Scrolling

If the material on a web page does not fit on to the screen then the visitor can use horizontal and vertical scrollbars to move around.

Vertical scrollbars are familiar to anyone who has used a word processing program. But it is still true that many visitors never scroll down a page, so most web designers place all the important information and links at the top of the home page. In Figure 1.5 there are links at the top of the page to the content that lies further down. This means that visitors can still access the content even if they are reluctant to scroll down.

Figure 1.5 Vertical scrollbar

Note:

Most visitors find horizontal scrollbars irritating. They sometimes appear when the web designer has not given enough thought to screen resolutions and window sizes.

Colour depth

In Figure 1.3 there is also a drop-down list to alter the colours. The options are:

- True Color (32 bit) – this gives millions of colours to choose from.
- High Color (16 bit) – this gives 65,536 different colours.
- 256 Colors (8 bit).
- 16 Colors.

True colour uses 32 bits (4 bytes) of memory to store the data about each pixel. Most screens today offer 32 bit colour. But when you design a web page you have to consider the needs of users who may be using lower colour settings.

Usability

Note:

Navigation refers to the way a visitor finds their way around a website, using links provided on the pages.

How often do you analyse the websites that you visit? By looking carefully at sites that you find attractive and easy to use, you can build up some general principles which will help you to design effective sites yourself. A website is practical for the typical visitor only if it is easy to read and easy to navigate.

Readability

As you look at sites ask yourself these questions:

- Is the language that is used easy to understand?
- Is the text large enough to read on my screen?
- Can I change the size of the text? On some sites this will have no effect, as the web designer will have fixed the size of the text.
- What colours have been used for the text and the background? Do these make it easy to read the text?
- Can I change the colours of the text and background? Again, on some sites this will have no effect, depending on whether the web designer has fixed the colours.

Task 1.2 — Changing the text size

Method

1   If you are using Internet Explorer, select the **View** menu, then select **Text Size**. Choose from Largest, Larger, Medium, Smaller and Smallest.

2   If you are using Netscape, select the **View** menu, then select **Text Zoom**. Choose from Smaller, Larger, or a percentage enlargement/reduction.

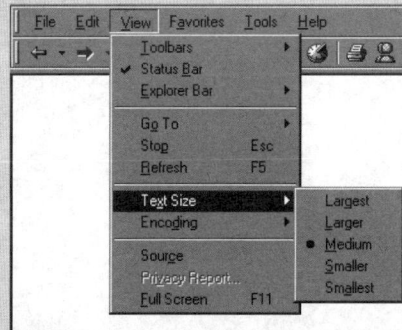

Figure 1.6 Changing text size in Internet Explorer

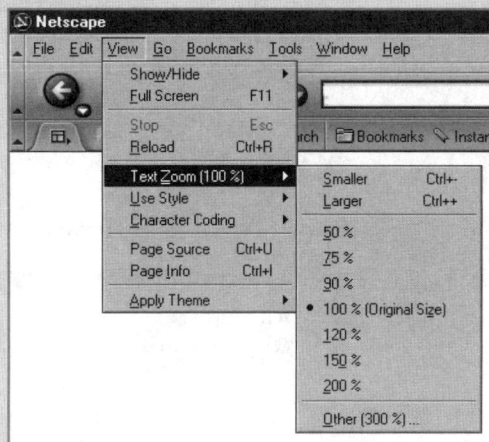

Figure 1.7 Changing text size in Netscape

Method

Note that these settings will change the appearance of all the applications that you use on your computer.

1. Select **Settings** and **Control Panel** in the **Start** menu.
2. Select **Display**, and in the dialogue box, click on the **Appearance** tab (Figure 1.8).
3. Choose from the colour schemes provided in the **Scheme** box.
4. You can change the colours of any of the elements and create your own colour scheme. The default text colour is normally black, but you can change this if you wish.
5. Alternatively, select **Settings** and **Control Panel** in the **Start** menu, then select **Desktop Themes**. This allows you to customise the appearance of the screen in many ways.

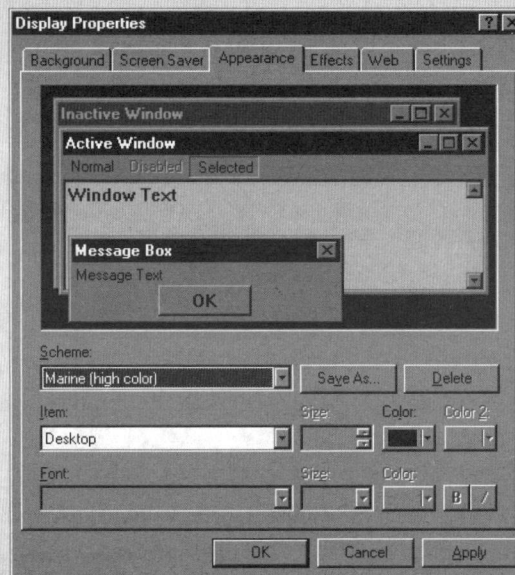

Figure 1.8 Using the Display Properties dialogue box to change appearance

Navigation

Now ask yourself these questions:

- How do I find other pages on the site? Are enough links provided on the home page?
- When I go to another page is it obvious how to get back to the home page?
- How are the links arranged on each page? Are they laid out as a menu, or are they embedded within the text?
- Is there a search box? Does it work as expected?

Speed of Internet connection

Users connect with the Internet using either a dial-up modem or a high speed broadband connection. The speed of the connection directly affects the time it takes for a page to be downloaded from a web server to the user's system. If a broadband connection is shared by many users on a network then the actual download speeds may be much slower than expected.

Web pages should be designed bearing in mind the needs of the users with the slowest connections. The typical dial-up modem runs at a speed of 56 kilobits per second, which is equivalent to 7 kilobytes per second. This is the maximum speed that can be achieved by the modem, depending on the amount of traffic going through the Internet Service Provider's servers, and in practice many dial-up connections are much slower than this.

When you download a web page you have to first of all download the actual page, which is a text file. The browser then interprets the code on the page, and downloads any images that are required. The images are stored as separate files on the server.

A typical simple web page may be 10 kilobytes in size and can download in a couple of seconds. The images on it can then take considerably longer to download. The process of requesting the image files itself adds extra time to the waiting period.

Browsers and HyperText Markup Language (HTML)

How a web browser displays a page

Web pages are stored as files written in HyperText Markup Language (HTML). The HTML code is interpreted by the browser and used to generate a web page.

A browser does a number of tasks:

- It sends a request for a page to the web server where the website is stored. The request identifies the page by its Uniform Resource Locator (URL) – often referred to as its web address. The HTML code for that page is then transmitted over the Internet.
- It interprets the HTML code and displays the web page.
- It sends requests to the web server for additional files that are referred to in the HTML code for the page – these could be for graphics or sounds. Each image or sound is transmitted as a separate file.
- When the user clicks on a hyperlink, it sends a new page request to the webserver.

Browsers have been updated to match the developments in HTML, but it is important to realise that not all users use the latest versions. Web pages can appear differently in different browsers and in different versions of the same browser (Figure 1.9).

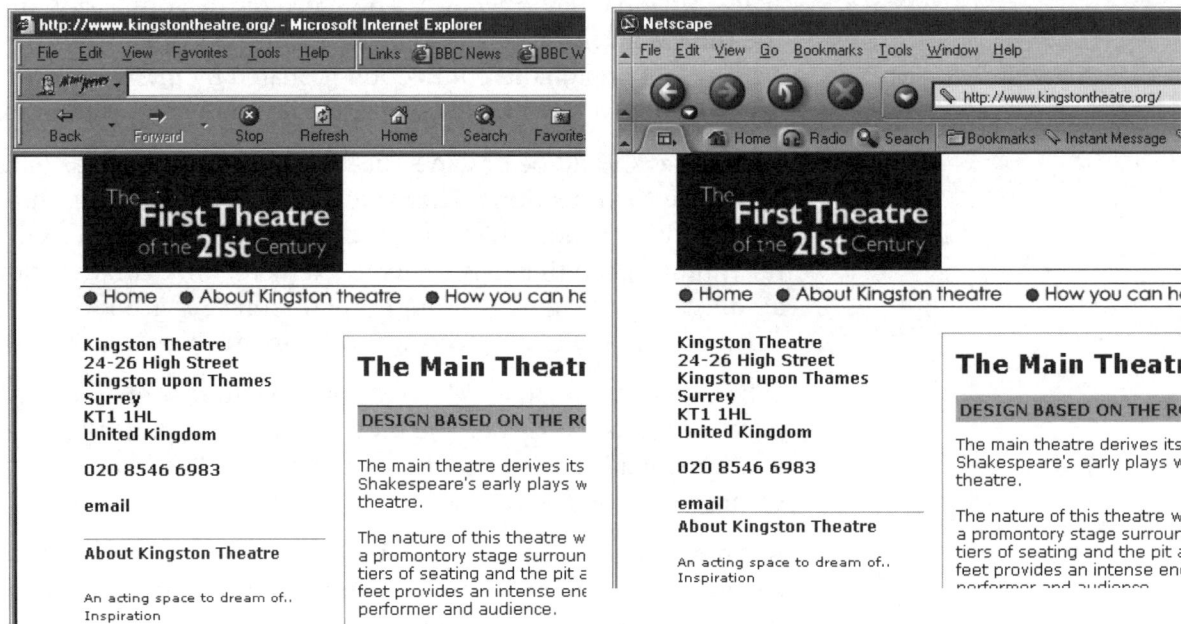

Figure 1.9 Spot the differences

HTML code

When you download a web page into a browser the HTML code is transferred to your computer. This is referred to as the source code. HTML code is always stored and transmitted in a text file (ASCII file). It usually has a file name with .htm or .html as its file extension, for example, information.htm

| Task 1.4 | Viewing HTML code for a web page |

Hint:

If you use a different browser, then you should also be able to view the source code from the **View** menu.

Method

1   In Internet Explorer, go to a suitable web page.
2   Select **View** then **Source**. This usually opens up Notepad and displays the code. Notepad is a text editor, and is the simplest means of viewing and creating text files.

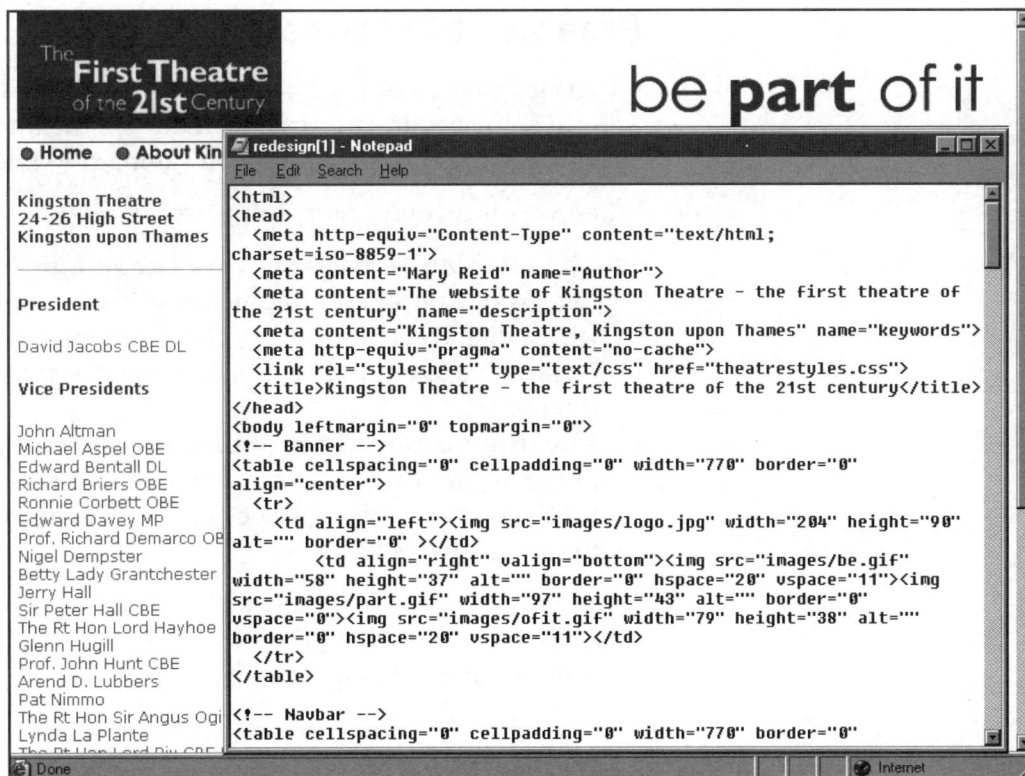

Figure 1.10 HTML code

Checking the files used on a web page

If you scan through a HTML file you will see references to other files that must be downloaded to complete the page. For example, you may see something like this:

```
<IMG src="http://www.thisismydomain.co.uk/pic.jpg" width=100 height=80 border=0 alt="My picture">
```

This tells the browser that it needs to download the picture stored as pic.jpg from the site www.thisismydomain.co.uk. You may also spot some links to other files that may be used, such as video or sound, or files that contain program code.

Graphics on the Web

Pixels

Note:

Some graphics software offers you the choice of measuring the image in cms or pixels – always choose pixels.

The screen resolution is measured in pixels. In addition, every graphical image is measured in pixels. When you are preparing an image for use on a web page you should always be aware of its dimensions in pixels.

You will also see that you can adjust many aspects of the layout of a page by referring to the size of areas in pixels, such as:

- The thickness of borders and lines.
- The width of cells in tables.
- The margins around a page.
- The spacing around an object.
- The width and height of frames.

Graphics file formats

All images have to be prepared for web use before they are inserted into a web page. Images are prepared by reducing them to the appropriate size, and by compressing them in one of the standard web formats.

When we use a computer graphic we can refer to its size in two senses:

- **The memory needed to store the image**. Most computer graphics use a very large amount of memory. For example, a photograph taken with a digital camera will be 2 MB or more. On a slow connection, a picture this size could take half an hour or more to download from the Internet!
- **The dimensions of the image measure in pixels**. It is very important that an image created for a web page is exactly the right size for the space it is going to occupy. This ensures that it has no more pixels than it really needs.

Because of the memory problems, all images used on websites are stored in a compressed format. Compression significantly reduces the amount of memory needed to store an image.

Information

Two compressed formats are commonly used on the Web:

- **jpg** – used mainly for photos, jpg (also referred to as jpeg) formatting gives photorealistic quality.
- **gif** – used for most other images, gif formatting is limited to 256 different colours.

The gif format usually takes up far less memory than the jpg format.

Figure 1.11 An example of an image in jpg format

Figure 1.12 An example of an image in gif format

Copyright issues

Writing, music, films and works of art are described as intellectual property, and the creators (or their employers) normally own the copyright to their work. This means that no-one else may copy, print, perform or film work without the copyright owner's permission. In Britain, copyright normally extends for 50 years after the creator's death, and the rights can extend to their heirs.

For many years it was not clear whether copyright extended to software products. The **Copyright, Designs and Patents Act, 1988** states that software (including websites) should be treated in the same way as all other intellectual property.

The copyright for a website belongs to the organisation that commissions it, not to the web designer.

Collecting and presenting information on websites

All content on a website should fall into one of these three categories:

- Material created within the organisation.
- Material used with the permission of the copyright owner.
- Copyright free.

Permission must be sought before using text, photographs, images, videos, music and other sounds that have originated elsewhere. This applies whether they are found on a website or in books or recordings. Software used on websites, such as scripts in Java, Visual Basic and other languages, as well as Flash animations, are also covered by copyright. The copyright holder will usually charge for permission to use their materials.

In general, it is wisest to assume that any material published in any format, including on the Web, is covered by copyright, unless it explicitly states that it is copyright free. **Copyright free** material is not necessarily cost free, but there are many sources of copyright free materials on the Web which can be downloaded and used at no charge.

> ## Information
>
> There are several terms used for software and other materials in relation to their copyright status.
> - **Shareware** is software that has been copyrighted by the originator, but is sold (or given) to users with permission to copy it and to share with others. Sometimes the conditions of use prevent the shareware from being used for commercial purposes. Shareware may be offered for free on an evaluation basis, but with payment required for continuing use. Many scripts are offered as shareware.
> - **Open source** software is software that can be distributed without restrictions, so that all users can view and modify the code. Open source software is not necessarily free of charge. Originally open source was known as free software in the sense of 'free to share' rather than 'at no cost'.
> - **Public domain** materials are items that are completely free of copyright and can be used by anyone.

→ Practise your skills 1

1 Find sources of copyright free, no cost, materials on the Web that can be used legally on a website. You could look for images, photos, animations, literature, articles and music.

→ Practise your skills 2

1 In the **Start** menu select **Settings** and then **Control Panel**.
2 Select **Display** and click on the Settings tab.
3 Write down the colour depth and screen area (resolution) that you are using. See what happens when you change these.
4 Launch your browser and try it out with different window sizes. Check whether the horizontal scroll bar appears.
5 Find the combination of resolution and window size that suits you best.
6 Change the default text size and see what effect it has on different websites.

→ Practise your skills 3

1 Visit several different types of website.
2 For each one that you visit, ask yourself:
   • Is the language that is used easy to understand?
   • How are the links arranged on each page? Are they laid out as a menu, or are they embedded within the text?
   • Is there a search box? Does it work as expected?

→ Practise your skills 4

1 Visit a website that you like.
2 Select a page that does not have too much material on it. Print out a screen shot of the page.
3 View the HTML code for the page. Print it out.
4 Look through the HTML code and try to relate the code to the contents of the page. Don't worry if you do not understand it all.

→ Check your knowledge

1 What is the resolution of a screen? List some of the resolutions commonly used.
2 Why is it unwise to use horizontal scrollbars when designing a website?
3 What is colour depth on a screen? What colour depth options are available?
4 How can you judge the usability of a website?
5 How does a browser find and display a web page?
6 Name the two most common image formats used on web pages.

Section 2

Creating a web page

You will learn to

- Achieve desired effects for:
  - ☐ Pages (set suitable default background page and text colours, background image)
  - ☐ Text (font, size, style and colour)
  - ☐ Paragraphs (paragraph and line breaks, indentation)

  by using:
  - ☐ A text editor to apply HTML tags
  - ☐ WYSIWYG HTML editing tools
- State the main features of the Hypertext Markup Language (HTML) and identify its limitations

Software for creating websites

Sections 2 and 3 offer an introduction to creating individual web pages, while Sections 6 to 11 describe some more advanced techniques that you can use which enable you to develop a fully functioning website.

Web authoring software

Web authoring packages, or web page generating software, provide facilities that are very similar to desktop publishing (DTP) packages, but geared to the specific demands of the Web. These packages give you a WYSIWYG (What You See Is What You Get) environment in which to develop web pages.

As you construct a web page in web authoring software, the package generates the HTML source code for you. This code can be edited directly. The HTML code can also be enhanced with scripts which create dynamic and other special effects.

You are free to look at the HTML code at any time, and to change or add to it directly. But it is perfectly possible to create a straightforward website that meets its purpose without knowing any HTML at all.

HTML editors

Hint:

If you are a beginner then you are strongly advised **not** to work directly in HTML editor, but to use the page layout facilities in web authoring software instead.

If you already have some experience of web authoring software then you may like to try writing HTML. You can do this in one of three ways:

1 **Using a text editor**. You can write HTML in a text editor such as Notepad. Each time you want to view the page you will have to save it with the file extension .htm or .html. You can then view the layout of the page by loading it into your browser.

2 **Using the HTML editor in web authoring software**. Most packages allow you to edit the HTML code, and then switch to the page layout option to see what it looks like. This is the best way to experiment with HTML.

3 **Using a specialist HTML editor**. There are a number of packages on the market that make it easy to write HTML code quickly and accurately. These include Macromedia Homesite, CoffeeCup HTML Editor and HTML-Kit.

Selecting an appropriate web authoring package

There are a number of useful web authoring packages available, such as Microsoft FrontPage and Macromedia Dreamweaver. Another simple web authoring package, Netscape Composer, can be downloaded free with the browser, Netscape. These packages provide you with a complete environment which helps to automate the process of linking pages together to form a complete website.

Most of these packages provide useful page templates that can be used to lay out the content. A beginner can use any of these, although to gain a real understanding of how web pages are built, it is better to start with a blank page.

Web authoring packages often provide wizards that can be used to create complete sites, with built in themed graphics and page layouts. Although some of the results can be quite pleasing, they are rather limiting. Websites produced in this way are sometimes difficult to modify and update, and they do look very similar to each other.

Finally, the templates and wizards in web authoring packages are very useful for creating quick design prototypes of sites, even if the final site is developed using more refined techniques.

Note:

To the right of the window you will see the **Task Pane** with a heading **New Page or Web**. You do not need this for now, so click on the close button (Figure 2.1).

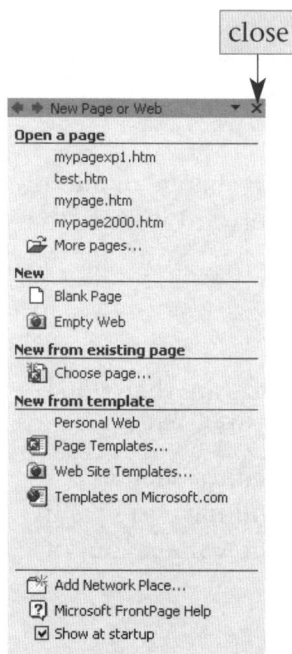

close

Figure 2.1 The Task Pane

Information

In this book all the case studies are based on Microsoft FrontPage XP, also known as FrontPage 2002. Similar features will be found in other web authoring packages.

Getting started

Task 2.1   Getting started with FrontPage

Method

1 When you launch Microsoft FrontPage, it usually opens with a blank page. If anything else is displayed instead, then click on **Page** in the **Views** bar (Figure 2.2, left hand side of the window).

2 Type in some text, as you would in a word processing program (Figure 2.2), and then save the page, giving it a suitable name. All standard web pages are saved with either .htm or .html as the filename extension.

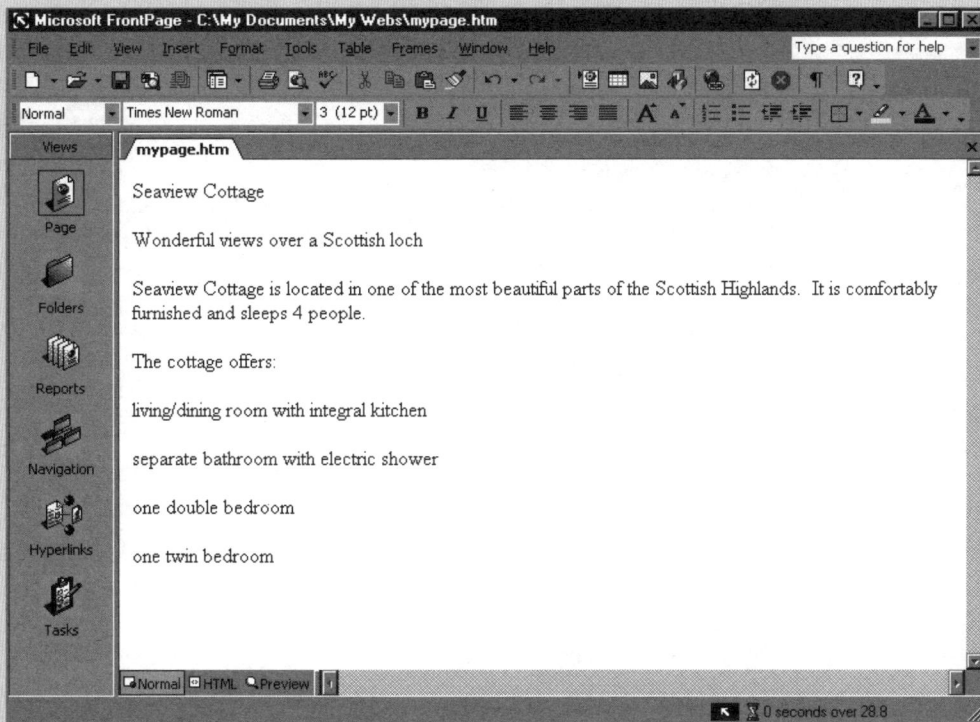

Figure 2.2 Entering text in page editor (Normal) mode in FrontPage

3   As in most word processing programs, pressing the **Enter** key starts a new paragraph, whereas pressing **Shift+Enter** starts a new line omitting the paragraph spacing.

4   FrontPage, like most web authoring packages, will allow you to display the page in three modes:
- Normal – page editor.
- HTML – shows the HTML code for the page.
- Preview – shows what the page will look like in a web browser.

5   You create the page in Normal mode, then you can check what it will look like when displayed by a browser in the Preview mode. At this stage they will look very similar, but differences will emerge as you use more advanced features.

Note:

Notice that the text wraps at the end of lines, just as it does in a word processing program.

Creating a web page

A web authoring environment includes a page editor and a HTML editor. As the page is developed in the page editor (Normal mode), the HTML code is automatically being generated in the background. Web designers can work in either editor and can easily switch between them.

The environment also provides a means of viewing the page in a browser. Some provide a built-in preview mode, which gives an immediate impression of how the page will be displayed. Some web design environments allow you to specify a standard browser that can be used for previewing the pages.

Information

There are some differences in the way different browsers (and different versions of the same browser) interpret HTML code, so it is important to check web pages in a range of standard browsers before they are published.

Understanding the HTML

The HTML code for a page could look like this:

```
<html>

<head>
<meta http-equiv="Content-Language" content="en-gb">
<meta http-equiv="Content-Type" content="text/html;
charset=windows-1252">
<meta name="GENERATOR" content="Microsoft FrontPage 5.0">
<meta name="ProgId" content="FrontPage.Editor.Document">
<title>New Page 1</title>
</head>

<body>

<p>Seaview Cottage</p>
<p>Wonderful views over a Scottish loch</p>
<p>Seaview Cottage is located in one of the most beautiful parts of
the Scottish Highlands.   It is comfortably furnished and
sleeps 4 people.</p>
<p>The cottage offers:</p>
<p>living/dining room with integral kitchen</p>
<p>separate bathroom with electric shower</p>
<p>one double bedroom </p>
<p>one twin bedroom</p>

</body>

</html>
```

The markup codes placed between triangular brackets are called **tags**. Tags are not case sensitive. Most tags come in pairs – the start tag (e.g. <p>) and the end tag (e.g. </p>).

This is the overall structure of the HTML code:

```
<html>

<head>

</head>

<body>

</body>

</html>
```

The HTML code, between the <html> and </html> tags, is divided into two sections. The head section holds information about the web page. The body section holds the actual contents of the web page.

Lines placed between the head tags are hidden from the visitor, but can be used very powerfully, as we will see later.

> ## Information
>
> - <p> and </p> mark the beginning and end of a paragraph.
> -   is an abbreviation for non-breaking space and is the code for a normal space character.
> -
 (not shown here) marks a line break.
>
> If you press the Tab (indent) key on the keyboard it simply adds a fixed number of non-breaking spaces to the text.

Using heading and paragraph styles

Hint:

You may be tempted to use the other options in the formatting toolbar, and introduce other fonts, but try to resist this for the moment.

The page editor allows you to highlight text and apply a style from a style list. This list is similar to the style list found in word processing packages, but is initially limited to a fixed set of styles. The list will always include Normal (or default), Heading 1 to Heading 6, plus bulleted and numbered list styles.

Figure 2.3 The style list in FrontPage

Task 2.2 Setting heading and paragraph styles

Method

In Normal mode, you can use pre-set styles with any of the text. The style list is found at the left end of the formatting toolbar, and the drop-down list displays the styles available (Figure 2.3).

1 Open the page saved in Task 2.1.

2 Highlight the lines of text in turn and apply the Heading 1, Heading 2 and Bulleted List styles from the style list as in Figure 2.4. (Normal is the default style for the page.)

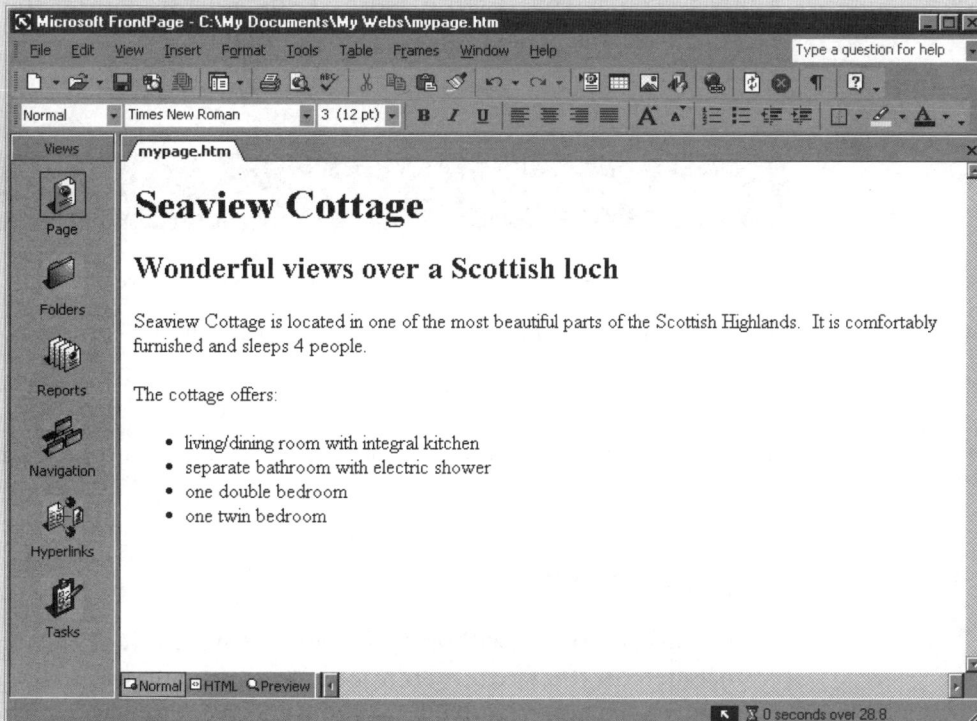

Figure 2.4 Headings and bulleted styles applied to the text

3 Check the HTML code to see what effect this has had.

4 In Normal mode try replacing the bulleted list style with the numbered list style, and then check the HTML code again.

5 You can edit the text in Normal mode if you want to create a specific web page. Don't forget to save your work before closing FrontPage.

The HTML code for the body of the page uses a different tag for each style.

```
<body>

<h1>Seaview Cottage</h1>
<h2>Wonderful views over a Scottish loch</h2>
<p>Seaview Cottage is located in one of the most beautiful parts of
the Scottish Highlands.  It is comfortably furnished and
sleeps 4 people.</p>
<p>The cottage offers:</p>
<ul>
<li>living/dining room with integral kitchen</li>
<li>separate bathroom with electric shower</li>
<li>one double bedroom </li>
<li>one twin bedroom</li>
</ul>

</body>
```

Information

- <h1>, <h2> etc. are the tags for Heading 1, Heading 2 etc. in the style list.
- <ul> marks the beginning of an unordered (i.e. unnumbered) list.
- <li> is a list item.

All tags, such as <p>, use the 'Normal' (default) style from the style list, except those that have been specially defined.

Formatting the text

There are several ways of formatting the text on a web page:

- Using text formatting options on the formatting toolbar.
- Using design themes.
- Creating user defined styles.

It is useful to know about all three methods, although the last method is by far the best.

Information

A visitor's browser will only be able to display a font that is already installed on the visitor's computer. So although a web designer may want to use an attractive but obscure font for a heading, the visitor will only be able to see the characters displayed in the font if they already have that font on their computer. If they do not have the required font then the browser will display the text in the default font for that browser; on a Microsoft Windows system the default font is normally Times New Roman, but the visitor can change the default font to whatever they wish.

Using the text formatting options on the formatting toolbar

In web authoring packages it is possible to highlight some text and use the formatting toolbar to format it, making a selection from fonts, font styles, text alignment and colours (Figure 2.5).

Unfortunately, if this method is used, every single paragraph and heading on every page of a website has to be individually formatted. This is a tedious process and some text can easily be overlooked. Worse still, if the web designer decides at some point to change the formatting, for example, to use a different colour for the main text, then every single instance has to be laboriously changed.

Task 2.3	Using text formatting options

Method

1   Open the file used in Task 2.2 and highlight the heading. On the **formatting** toolbar, use the **Font**, **Font Size**, and **Font Color** buttons to format the text.
2   Highlight other sections of text and format those. Don't forget to save your work before closing FrontPage.

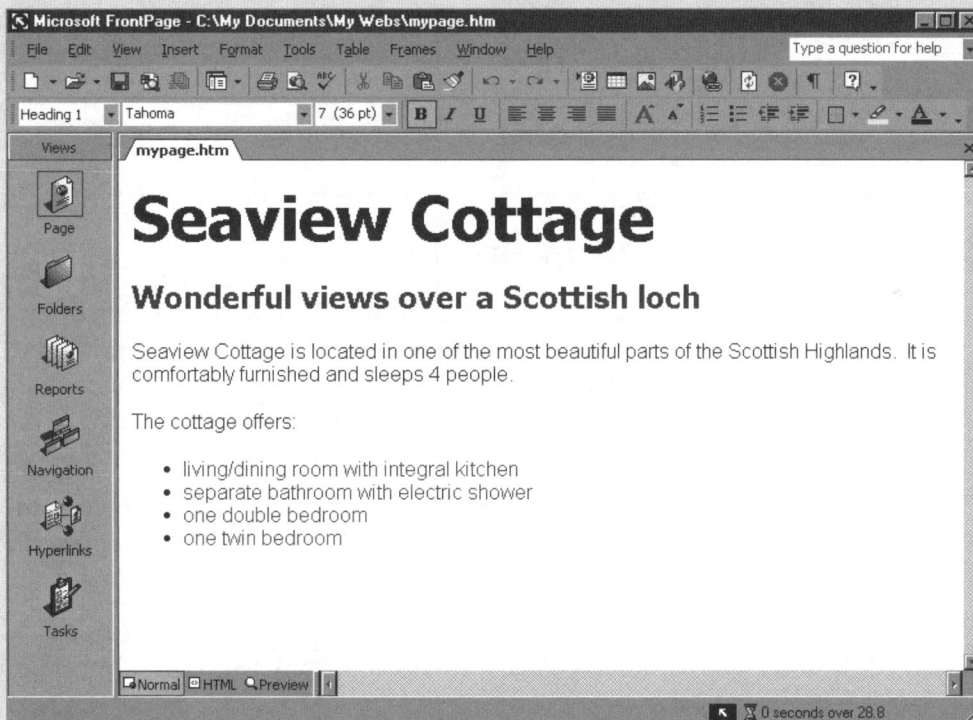

Figure 2.5 A formatted page

This is the HTML code for the body of the page shown in Figure 2.5:

```
<body>

<h1><font face="Tahoma" color="#0000FF" size="7">Seaview
Cottage</font></h1>
<h2><font face="Tahoma" color="#008000">Wonderful views over a
Scottish loch</font></h2>
<p><font face="Arial" color="#0000FF">Seaview Cottage is
located in one of the most beautiful parts of the Scottish
Highlands. It is comfortably furnished and sleeps 4 people.
</font></p>
<p><font face="Arial" color="#0000FF">The cottage offers:
</font></p>
<ul>
<li><font face="Arial" color="#FF0000">living/dining room with
integral kitchen</font></li>
<li><font face="Arial" color="#FF0000">separate bathroom with
electric shower</font></li>
<li><font face="Arial" color="#FF0000">one double bedroom
</font></li>
<li><font face="Arial" color="#FF0000">one twin bedroom
</font></li>
</ul>

</body>
```

Information

- <font> includes all the font properties that apply up to the </font> tag.

Using design themes

FrontPage and other web authoring packages provide you with pre-designed themes that can be applied across a website. These themes initially look pleasing, so they are very popular, especially on personal websites. They do appear again and again on the Web though, so it is not advisable to use them, unmodified, for serious web development.

However, you can modify most elements within a theme, and you can use this technique to give an acceptable and distinctive appearance to a simple website.

When you use a theme, the HTML may not appear to change much. For example, in FrontPage a theme is simply referenced by a tag in the head like this:

```
<meta name="Microsoft Theme" content="sumipntg 011">
```

However, this is a bit misleading as FrontPage does insert formatting codes when the page is uploaded to the server.

| Task 2.4 | Using a FrontPage theme |

Method

1   Open the page used in Task 2.3.
2   Remove the text formatting by selecting **Select All** from the **Edit** menu, then **Remove Formatting** from the **Format** menu.
3   Reapply the Heading 1 and Heading 2 styles to the headings as before.
4   Select **Format**, then **Theme**. Browse through the themes and select one. You will be impressed by the immediate improvement to your page. Figure 2.6 shows an example theme in use.
5   You can modify any of the elements of a theme by clicking on **Modify** in the **Themes** dialogue box.
6   Don't forget to save your work before closing FrontPage. You may be asked to **Save Embedded Files**. If so, click on OK.

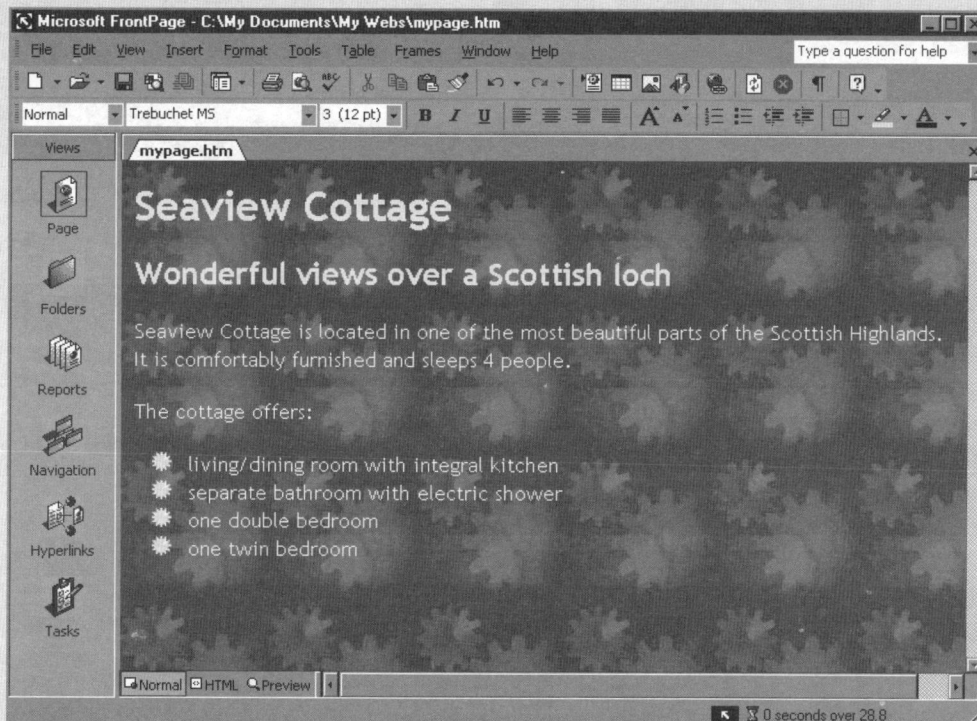

Figure 2.6 Using a FrontPage theme

Hint:

You can go back to the Themes dialogue box to change a theme at any time.

Creating user defined styles

FrontPage themes are useful for personal or very simple sites, but should not be used for professional websites. Instead, you can define the styles for each of the styles that you use from the style list.

This process adds to the HTML code a list of the styles that you have defined. A list of user defined styles is known as a style sheet.

Method

1. Open the page used in Task 2.4.
2. Remove the theme from the page by selecting **Format**, then **Theme**.
3. Select **No theme** from the list of themes. It should now look like Figure 2.4 again.
4. Select **Format** then **Style**. In the **Style** dialogue box (Figure 2.7), select the h1 (Heading 1) tag from the **Styles** list. Click on **Modify**.

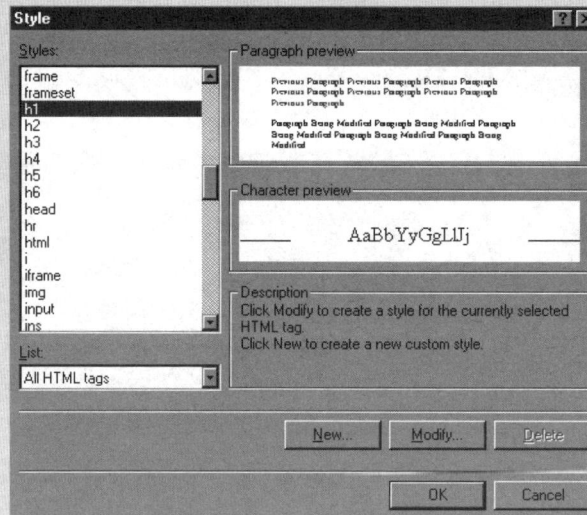

Figure 2.7 The Style dialogue box

5. In the **Modify Style** dialogue box (Figure 2.8), click on **Format**, then select **Font**.

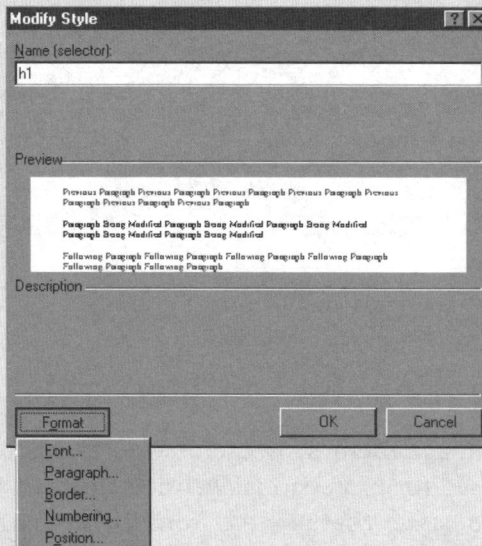

Figure 2.8 Modifying a style

6   In the **Font** dialogue box (Figure 2.9), select from the font options that you want for h1, then click on OK.

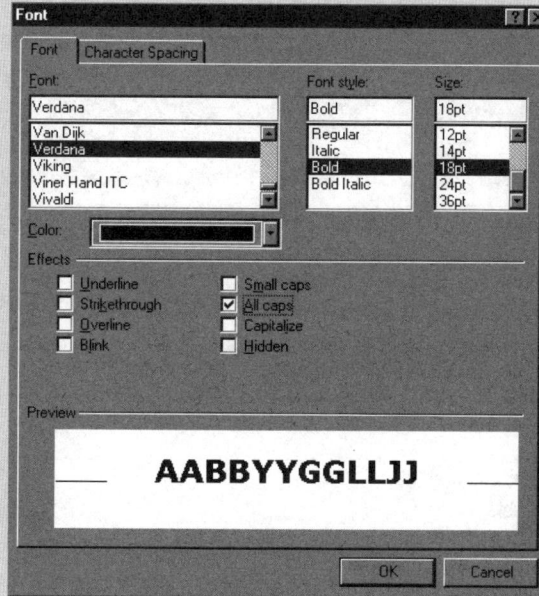

Figure 2.9 The Font dialogue box

7   Back in the **Modify Style** dialogue box, click on **Format**, then explore the other formatting options open to you.

8   When you have defined one style, you will see h1 listed as a user defined style.

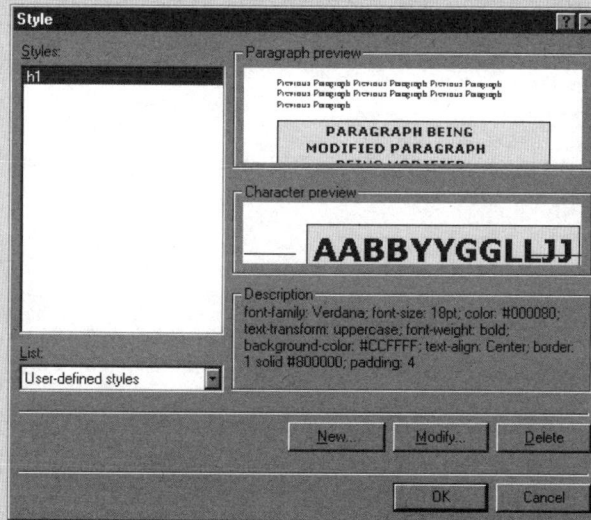

Figure 2.10 A user defined style

9 To define another style, click on **List:** and select **All HTML tags.** Find the tag you want to define and repeat the process. Don't forget to format the styles for p and li.

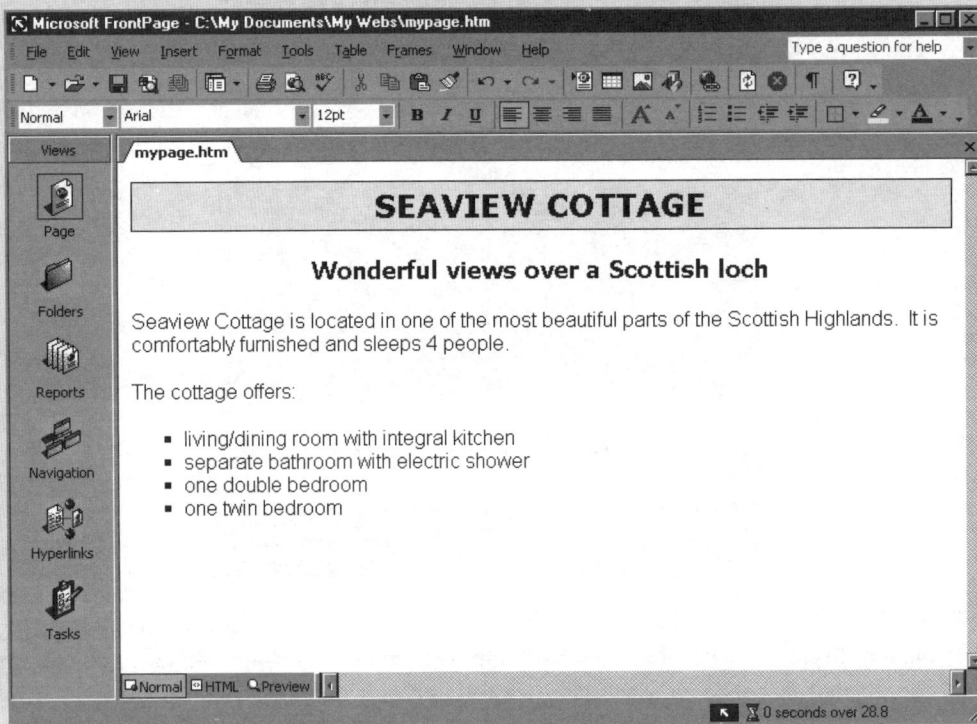

Figure 2.11 A web page with user defined styles

The HTML for the page with user defined styles looks like this:

```
<head>
<meta http-equiv="Content-Language" content="en-gb">
<meta http-equiv="Content-Type" content="text/html;
charset=windows-1252">
<meta name="GENERATOR" content="Microsoft FrontPage 5.0">
<meta name="ProgId" content="FrontPage.Editor.Document">
<title>New Page 1</title>
<meta name="Microsoft Theme" content="none">
<style>
<!--
h1 { font-family: Verdana; font-size: 18pt; color: #000080; text-
transform: uppercase; font-weight: bold; background-color:
#CCFFFF; text-align: Center; border: 1 solid #800000; padding: 4 }
h2 { font-family: Tahoma; font-size: 14pt; color: #800000; text-
align: Center;font-weight: bold }
p { font-family: Arial; font-size: 12pt; color: #000080 }
li { font-family: Arial; font-size: 12pt; color: #000080; text-
align: Left; list-style-type: square }
-->
</style>
</head>

<body>

<h1>Seaview Cottage</h1>
<h2>Wonderful views over a Scottish loch</h2>
<p>Seaview Cottage is located in one of the most beautiful parts of
the Scottish Highlands.  It is comfortably furnished and
sleeps 4 people.</p>
```

```
<p>The cottage offers:</p>
<ul>
<li>living/dining room with integral kitchen</li>
<li>separate bathroom with electric shower</li>
<li>one double bedroom </li>
<li>one twin bedroom</li>
</ul>

</body>

</html>
```

The code between the <style> tags lists the chosen styles for each tag. This code is known as an embedded style sheet. You can edit this directly in HTML if you like.

Information

A style sheet opens up many more possibilities, some of which are explored in Sections 7 and 10. Style sheets can be used with any web development software, but Themes are specific to the software that you use to make your website.

Viewing your page in a browser

The Preview mode in FrontPage lets you check how the page will appear eventually. But it is always useful to view it in a browser, in order to see it as a visitor would see it.

Task 2.6 — Viewing a page in a browser

Method

1. Open your page in FrontPage. If you make any changes to it, you should save the page again before viewing it in a browser.
2. In the **File** menu select **Preview in Browser**. The Preview in Browser dialogue box lists any browsers on your system that have already been identified to FrontPage.
3. If no browsers are shown, or you want to use a different one from the one listed, click on **Add**. Browse to the program file for the browser you want to use.
4. Select the browser from those listed in the Preview in Browser dialogue box. Select the resolution that you want to use, then click Preview.
5. The browser window opens with your page displayed.

Hint:

If you are not sure where the program file for a browser is located then find a shortcut to the browser. Shortcuts can be found on the desktop, or in **Programs** on the **Start** menu. Right-click on a shortcut to the browser, select **Properties**, select the **Shortcut** tab, then note the file address given as the **Target**.

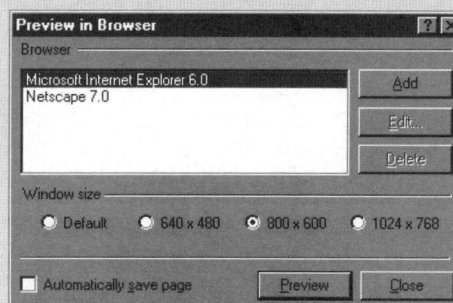

Figure 2.12 The Preview in Browser dialogue box

→ Practise your skills 1

1 Launch your web authoring software.
2 Create your own web page. This could give personal information about you, your work and your interests. Alternatively it could be a page where you can share news with friends and family overseas.
3 Use the styles from the style list for headings and subheadings.
4 Apply a design theme to the page.
5 Look at the HTML code for the page.
6 Be web safe, and do not include your home address or phone number on the page.

→ Practise your skills 2

1 Go back to the web page and HTML code that you printed for the Practise your skills task in Section 1.
2 Look through the HTML code and see if you recognise any more elements.

→ Practise your skills 3

1 Create a new web page for a community organisation or small business.
2 Use the styles from the style list for headings and subheadings.
3 Create user defined styles for the page.
4 View your page in a browser.

→ Check your knowledge

1 What is web authoring software?
2 In HTML, what is a tag?
3 What happens to the HTML code when you use the text formatting options?
4 What is the advantage in using FrontPage design themes over text formatting?
5 What are user defined styles?

Section 3

Using images and tables on a web page

You will learn to

- Convert images into formats suitable for inclusion on web pages
- Use tables to enhance layout of text and graphics

Hint:

If you want to create a small image it is sometimes helpful to design a larger image then reduce it in size. Once you have designed your image you should reduce the dimensions (number of pixels) to the exact ones needed on the web page.

Images for web pages

Create an image in a graphics package

There are many ways of finding or creating images to use on a website. You can use a simple package like Microsoft Paint or a more sophisticated one like Adobe Illustrator. You will be saving it in gif format, which uses only 256 colours, so you should only use the preset colours that are offered to you.

Task 3.1   Creating a small image for a web page in Microsoft Paint

Method

1   Launch Paint.
2   Select **Attributes** in the **Image** menu. Set the page size at 100 pixels by 100 pixels.
3   Draw a simple image, like the sprig of heather shown in Figure 3.1.
4   Select **Stretch and Skew** from the **Image** menu. Reduce both height and width to 25%.
5   Save the image. In the **Save as Type** box select **Graphics Interchange Format (*.gif)** as shown in Figure 3.2.

The image can now be used as a small icon or bullet.

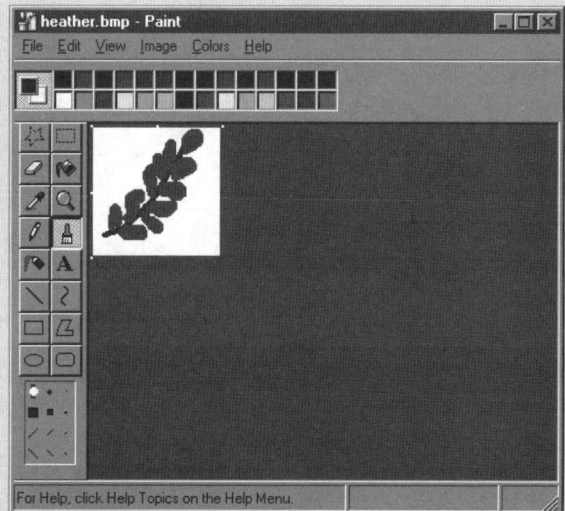

Figure 3.1 An image created in Paint

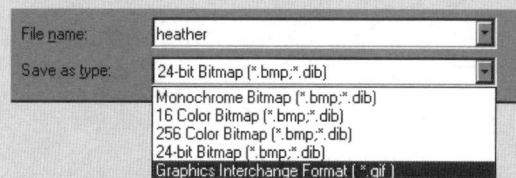

Figure 3.2 Saving an image in gif format

Use a photograph

You can either take a photo with a digital camera or scan in a photo print. This will normally be stored as a bitmap (.bmp), which is a non-compressed pixel format. You can then open it in a photo manipulation package, such as Microsoft Photo Editor.

If you take a photo from a photo CD that was supplied when a camera film was developed, the images will normally be in jpg format already. You will probably need to reduce the dimensions of the photo to something between 100 and 300 pixels wide. Save the image as a jpg again.

Task 3.2	Preparing a photo for use on a web page

Method

1 Open an existing digital photo in Microsoft Photo Editor as shown in Figure 3.3.
2 Select **Resize** from the **Image** menu.
3 Reduce the % width and % height by the same amount. Experiment until the width of the image in pixels is suitable for display on the web page.
4 Save the photo using the jpg format.

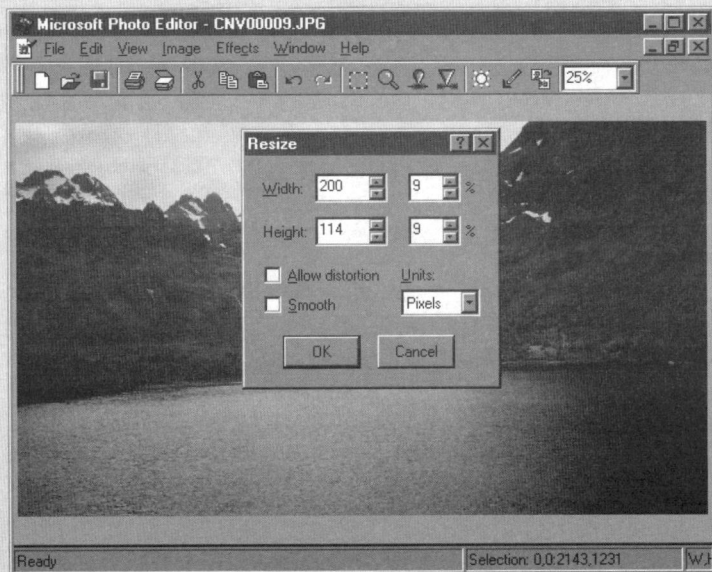

Figure 3.3 A photo being manipulated in Microsoft Photo Editor

Hint:

Make sure that the units are displayed in pixels.

Obtain an image from the Web

You should never simply copy images from existing websites because they will probably be protected by copyright. Fortunately though, there are numerous sources of copyright-free images online. Note that in many cases the creators require you to acknowledge the source of any image you use.

Weblinks:

To access the website content relevant to this page visit www.heinemann.co.uk/hotlinks

Enter express code 2563P, click GO and then click on the relevant link from the text.

Hint:

Before you add an image to the page, check that it has the correct dimensions, in pixels, and does not take up too much memory.

Information

A search in a search engine will produce a bewildering choice of sites offering copyright free images online, but you might like to start with the Freefoto and Freegraphics websites. Links to these sites are available on the Heinemann hotlinks web page as ref29a (Freefoto) and ref29b (Freegraphics).

Adding an image to the page

You can add an image to the page, provided it is already in jpg or gif format. Some web authoring packages, such as FrontPage, will convert the images for you, but it is often better to retain control over the process yourself.

Task 3.3 — Adding an image

Method

1 In FrontPage open the page that you were working on in Section 2.
2 In Normal view click at the position on the page where you want to place an image.
3 Select **Insert**, **Picture**, then **From File**. Find and select the prepared image. Don't forget to save your work before closing FrontPage.

Figure 3.4 Adding a photo to a page

Adding a horizontal line and a background colour

A **horizontal line** can be added to the page, usually using the Insert menu on a web authoring package. The tag for this is simply **<hr>**, for horizontal rule, and there is no end tag in this case. The colour of the line can be set up in a style sheet, and will apply to all the lines you insert.

The **colour of the background** can be changed. This can be done through a Page Properties dialogue box, but in general it is better to do it through the Style dialogue box.

Most web authoring packages offer a palette of colours. The HTML adds the 'bgcolor' attribute to the <body> tag.

```
<body bgcolor="#FFFF00">
```

Information

- bgcolor gives the background colour, with the value expressed either as a six digit hexadecimal code, e.g. #FFFF00, or as a RGB code, e.g. rgb(255, 255, 0), or as a standard colour word, e.g. yellow.

Task 3.4   Adding lines and a background

Method

1   Open the page used in Task 3.3.
2   In FrontPage, select **Horizontal Line** from the **Insert** menu to add a standard grey line that extends across the page.
3   Select **Style** from the **Format** menu to change the colour of any lines you insert. Select the hr tag. Use the **Border** option and select the **Shading** tab. The **Foreground** colour will give the colour of the line.
4   To change the colour of the background on a page, select **Style** from the **Format** menu, then select the body tag. Again, use the **Border** option and select the **Shading** tab. Save your work before closing FrontPage.

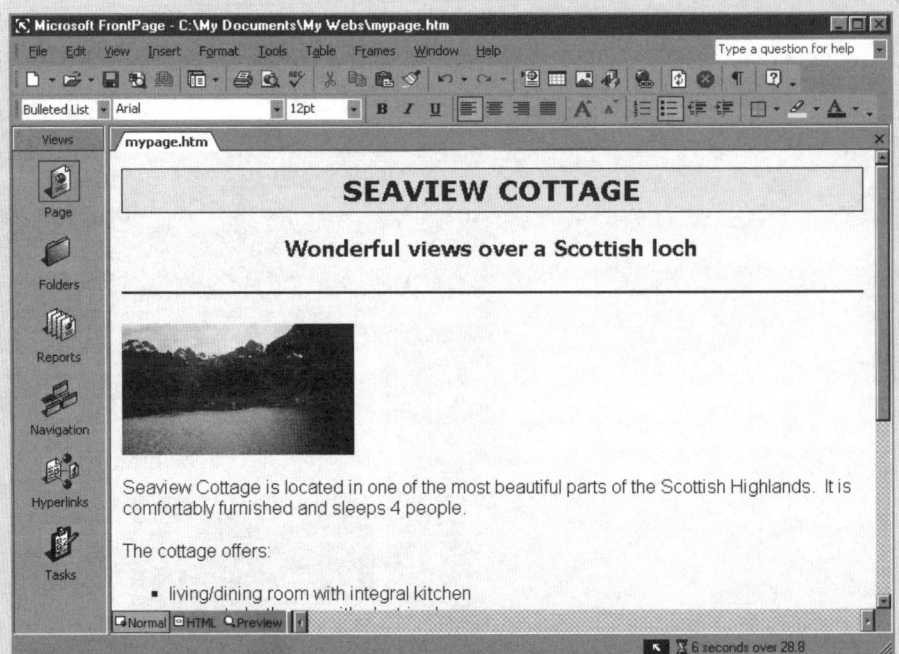

Figure 3.5 Background and a horizontal line inserted

Hint:

Do not use the picture properties to change the width or height properties of the image. If you want to change the size of an image then go back to your graphics software, or use the resampling facility in FrontPage which is described later.

Using the picture properties

Every image on a web page has a number of properties. These include the alignment of the image (left, right or centre), the thickness of the border, and the horizontal spacing (to the sides) and vertical spacing (above and below) around it. The border and spacing properties are measured in pixels. The width and height of the image are also properties.

Task 3.5 — Changing the picture properties of an image

Method

1 In Normal view right-click on the image, and select **Picture Properties**.
2 Set the **Alignment** to **Right**.
3 Set the **Horizontal spacing** to 10 pixels as shown in Figure 3.6.
4 The image should position itself as shown in Figure 3.7.

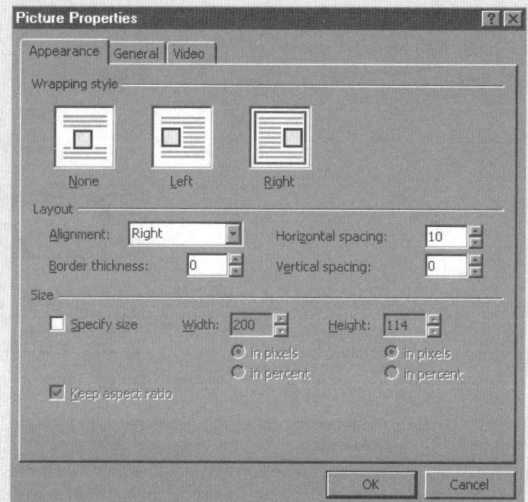

Figure 3.6 Setting the picture properties in FrontPage

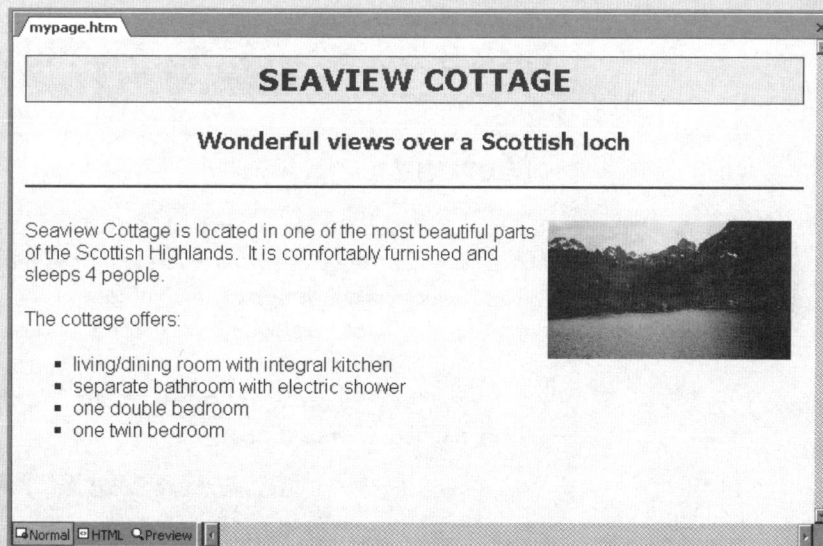

Figure 3.7 Using picture properties to layout a page

Information

The gif that you designed in Paint had a white background. If you add it to the page, you will find that it looks odd against the coloured background of the page. You have three options:

1 Change the background of the page back to white.
2 Change the background of the image to the same colour as the page.
3 Use a special property of gifs that allows you to make the background of the gif transparent (see Section 8).

Figure 3.8 Images with the wrong background colour

Tables on web pages

Tables can be created on a web page, just as they can in a word processing program. A table can be used for tabulation – to display data in boxes in the traditional way.

Tables are more commonly used on web pages as a way of arranging text and images on screen.

Web authoring packages provide dialogue boxes for creating tables, usually from the Table menu.

Task 3.6 — Creating a table to display data

Method

1   Open the page used in Task 3.4.
2   Click on the page where you want the table to appear.
3   Select **Table**, **Insert**, then **Table**.
4   In the **Table** dialogue box, enter 3 as the number of rows, and 2 as the number of columns.
5   Set the Alignment to **Center**. Enter 1 as the border size and 5 as the cell padding (Figure 3.9).

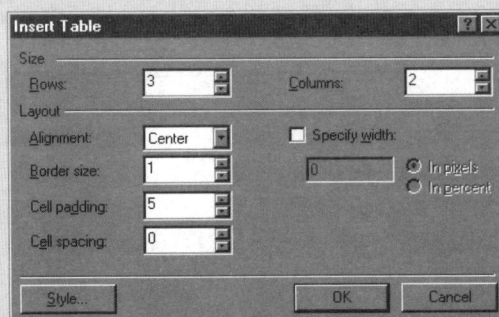

Figure 3.9 Setting up a table

6   An outline of the table appears on the page. Start entering the data in the table, as shown in Figure 3.10

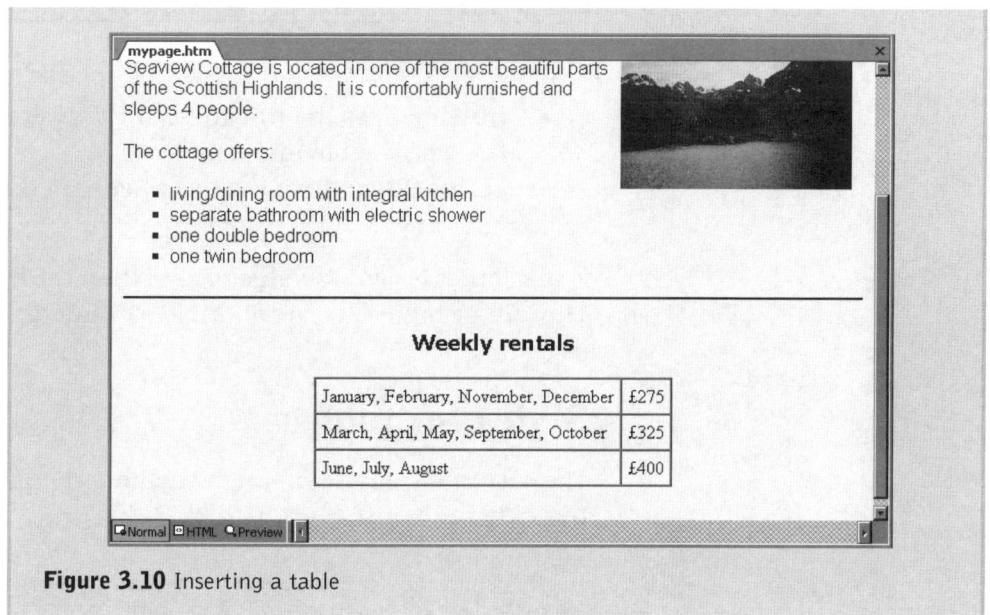

Figure 3.10 Inserting a table

Table properties

It is useful to see how the HTML handles tables and their properties. The HTML code for a table has this basic structure:

```
<table>
<tr>
<td> </td>
<td> </td>
</tr>
<tr>
<td> </td>
<td> </td>
</tr>
<tr>
<td> </td>
<td> </td>
</tr>
</table>
```

This table consists of three rows each with a **<tr>** tag. Each row has two cells each with a **<td>** tag (for table data).

This shows the HTML code for the table shown in Figure 3.10.

```
<table border="1" cellpadding="5" cellspacing="0">
<tr>
<td>January, February, November, December</td>
<td>£275</td>
</tr>
<tr>
<td>March, April, May, September, October</td>
<td>£325</td>
</tr>
<tr>
<td>June, July, August</td>
<td>£400</td>
</tr>
</table>
```

The <table> tag can take a number of attributes.

Information

- **border** fixes the thickness of the border around the perimeter of the whole table in pixels.
- **cellpadding** fixes the space between the border and the text in pixels.

If the border is given a value of zero then the borders of all the cells disappear. This can be used to create an invisible structure for laying out items on a web page.

Styles for tables

The text in the table will be in the underlying default style. You can define the style in the usual way.

Task 3.7 Defining the style of the text in the table

Method

1 You can set the style for the table by selecting **Style** from the **Format** menu.

2 In the **Style** dialogue box select **All HTML tags** in the **List** box. Select the table tag. Click on **Modify** to define the style for the text in the table.

Weekly rentals

January, February, November, December	£275
March, April, May, September, October	£325
June, July, August	£400

Figure 3.11 Style defined for a table

Cell properties

Individual cells in a table can be given their own properties, as in:

```
<td align="center" valign="top">
```

Information

- **align** is the horizontal alignment (the default value is 'left').
- **valign** is the vertical alignment, in this case placing the contents of the cell at the top (the default value is 'middle').

Task 3.8 Setting the properties for a cell

Method

1 Right-click inside a cell. Select **Cell Properties**.

2 Make your own choice of properties for the cell.

→ Practise your skills 1

1 Launch Microsoft Paint (or other painting software).
2 Set the page size at 200 by 100 pixels.
3 Create an image that you can use on one of your web pages. Reduce it in size if necessary.
4 Save the image as a gif.
5 Insert the image on the page.
6 Right-click on the image and select **Picture Properties**. Explore the options that it offers.

→ Practise your skills 2

1 Launch Microsoft Photo Editor (or other photo editing software).
2 Find and load a digital photo. Change the size of the photo.
3 Explore the other options offered by the software.
4 Save the image as a jpg.
5 Insert the photo on one of the pages that you created.

→ Practise your skills 3

1 Use a search engine on the Internet, such as Google, to find sources of copyright free images that you can use.
2 Download some images that you would like to use.
3 Check the conditions of use for the images.

→ Practise your skills 4

1 Set up a table on the pages that you created for a community group or small business.
2 Enter useful information in the table, such as the prices of goods, or the dates of events.
3 Define styles for the table.

→ Check your knowledge

1 How can you find a digital photo to use on a website?
2 What is photo manipulation?
3 In FrontPage, what can you change or set in the Picture Properties dialogue box?
4 What are the two main uses of tables on a web page?

Section 4 — User requirements analysis

Like any other software project, the development of a website must be taken through the usual stages of analysis, design, implementation and evaluation (review). User interfaces, which are of particular importance in websites, are usually developed using user-centred design methods.

You are going to act as a web designer, and as such should work through the project stages in some detail.

User-centred design

User-centred design is an approach to the design and implementation of software, especially the user interface, which involves the user at every stage of the project. At the design stage, a prototype is created which the user reviews. Alternative designs are then developed in response to their feedback.

The design process usually follows this pattern:

- **User requirements analysis**, which leads to a design specification. Through interviews with the client, the designer must establish the purpose of the website and the target audience, and then create a design for the project.
- **Prototyping** and **implementation**.
- **Technical testing** and **publishing**.
- **Evaluation** against specification.

In this section you will look in detail at the first stage, with some comments on the prototyping process.

Functions of websites

The first task you need to do within user requirements analysis is to establish the purpose and function of your proposed website.

Websites can be developed for a variety of purposes, and many sites have more than one purpose.

- **To inform** – all websites provide some information, which is one reason why the Internet became known as the Information Superhighway.
- **To promote and sell** – websites can be used to promote products and services to visitors.
- **To interact** – websites can easily offer interactivity, allowing the visitor to send information and ideas back to the organisation and engage in dialogue.

E-commerce is the term used to describe sites that offer online sales.

Types of website

> **Note:**
>
> We sometimes talk about 'communities of place' (based around a geographical area) and 'communities of interest' (based around a shared interest). The Web contains many communities of interest, within which the members may be widely spread geographically.

Websites can be developed by a number of different types of organisations. Each will have their own combinations of purposes. For example:

- Educational organisations create websites to inform and interact. One of the earliest uses of the Internet was by universities to disseminate academic papers.
- Governmental and other public service organisations create websites to inform the public, and increasingly to provide a space where citizens can interact with decision makers.
- Commercial organisations use websites to promote themselves and also to offer online selling.
- Community organisations use websites to inform people and to interact. Some communities exist entirely within the Internet.

Using a website to inform

Websites are an ideal means of providing information, so it is not surprising that some of the most visited sites are those that specialise in giving information to the general public. These include the traditional media such as newspapers and magazines, which have developed their own online versions, and television and radio channels. Whilst it is possible to listen to radio and watch television over the Internet, these sites have taken on a life of their own, exploiting the specific qualities of the new medium.

Case study – BBCi

B B C i

Figure 4.1 BBCi's site is used for external communication

BBCi has become a channel in its own right and does not simply repeat material broadcast by the BBC. In addition to live radio and streaming video, it provides interactive features such as webchats and message boards, as well as up-to-date information on a huge variety of subjects. It is the most visited website in the UK. A link to the BBCi website is available on the Heinemann hotlinks web page as ref38a.

You might also like to look at the BBC iCan website which offers information and guidance for you to start a campaign, or join an existing one, about something that concerns you. A link to this website is available on the Heinemann hotlinks web page as ref38b.

Weblinks:

To access the website content relevant to this page visit www.heinemann.co.uk/hotlinks

Enter express code 2563P, click GO and then click on the relevant link from the text.

Many public services have sites, such as the much-used NHS-Direct website, that specialise in communicating information to members of the public. There are also a few online organisations that have built huge databases of articles and external links, which they then provide as service to visitors. One example of this is the About website. Links to these two sites are available on the Heinemann hotlinks web page as ref38c (NHS-Direct) and ref38d (About).

Information

You may wonder how an organisation can finance a free information service. You will usually find that sites are sponsored by other businesses and their advertisements will appear in banners and popup screens. Some information sites, such as the Government's DirectGov (Heinemann hotlinks ref38e), are paid for out of public taxation.

Using a website to promote and sell

Many websites promote a service or product but without actually offering online sales. For example, most rock bands have websites which promote the band and their music, although visitors may not be able to buy albums directly from the site.

Many tourist attractions use the Internet to give people information about location and opening times and to encourage people to attend. Similarly, hotels often provide basic information even though you may have to phone them to book a room.

Case study – Disneyland Resort, Paris

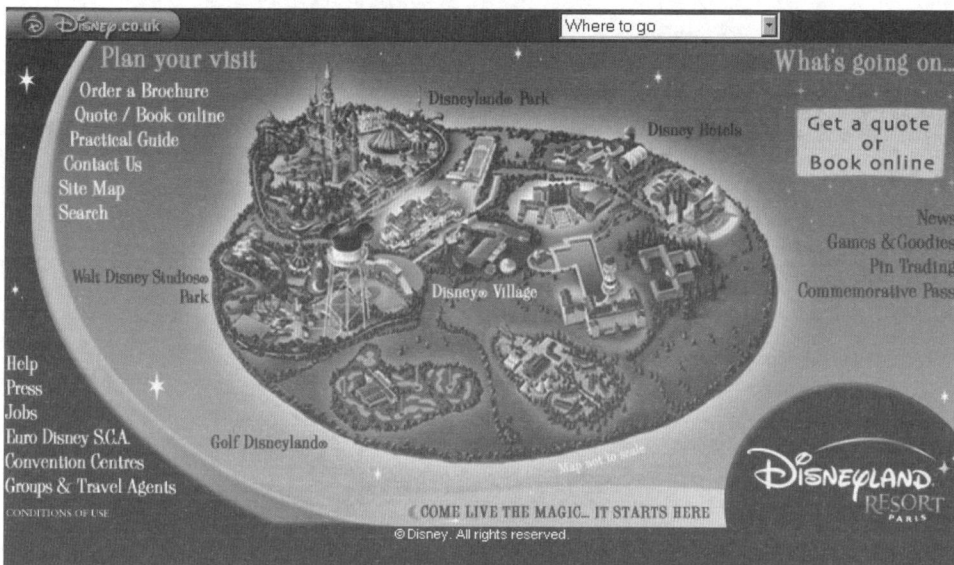

Figure 4.2 Marketing Disneyland Resort Paris

Disneyland Resort Paris uses its website to show what it offers and to encourage people to visit. Can you find other leisure attractions that market their services on the Internet?

Here are some other organisations that use the Internet for promotion:

- Schools, colleges and universities.
- Charities.
- Political parties.
- Churches and other religious organisations.
- Theatres and cinemas.

All these organisations are trying to persuade the visitor to do something in response and are not simply providing interesting information. Some promotional sites also offer online sales, and start to develop an e-commerce angle. The dividing line between promotion and e-commerce sites is not precise; the category depends on what the main purpose of the site is.

Information

As the Internet has grown, so more and more businesses have emerged that exist only on the Internet. There are many examples of online banks, shops, travel agencies and insurance companies. These companies sell goods and services directly to the customer.

Customers normally pay for products online with a credit card, and they need to be reassured that their payments will be safe. Online payments are usually routed through a secure server which encrypts all the data. More information about this is given in Section 13.

Goods have to be sent to the customer either by post or using a distribution company, and successful online businesses usually guarantee to deliver goods within 24 hours or a few days.

Case study – Amazon, the online bookstore

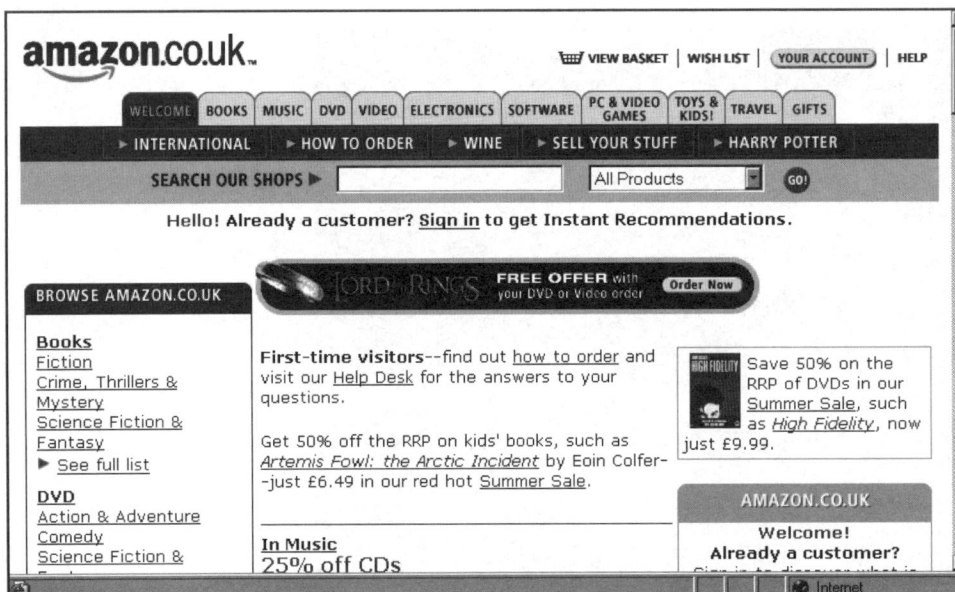

Figure 4.3 Amazon's e-commerce site

Amazon describes the company in this way:

'Who We Are

Amazon.co.uk is the trading name for Amazon.com Int'l Sales, Inc. and Amazon.com International Auctions, Inc. Both companies are subsidiaries of Amazon.com – a leading online retailer of products that inform, educate and inspire. The Amazon group also has stores in the United States, Germany, France, Japan and Canada. Amazon.co.uk has its origins in an independent online store, Bookpages, which was established in 1996, and subsequently acquired by Amazon.com in early 1998.

What We Do

Amazon.co.uk offers a catalogue of more than 1.5 million books, thousands of CDs, DVDs and videos, a wide range of software and PC & video games and a great selection of children's products in Toys & Kids! The site also hosts online auctions and brings independent buyers and sellers together in zShops, our online marketplace. In addition, customers have access to a variety of other resources including customer reviews, emailed personal recommendations and gift certificates.'

Source: Amazon website

Some Internet businesses offer services, which avoids the need to deliver goods. For example, online banking has grown very rapidly, and customers can view their balance, make payments and generally manage their accounts at any time of the day. Similarly, travel companies can send documents, such as ticket confirmations, by email and may not need to use the post at all. In addition, many high street chains now have online e-commerce operations as well. Large supermarkets offer a home shopping service which can be very helpful for people who are housebound, have young children, or lead busy lives.

Target audience

User analysis for a website includes an assessment of the target audience. The intended audience may be the public in general, or it may be targeted at specified age bands (children, the elderly), communities of interest (members of a club, people who enjoy a leisure activity, researchers, political and pressure groups), geographical communities, shoppers, travellers etc. Most sites are built with a typical visitor in mind.

One particular consideration is whether the site is intended for internal use only – by members of a company or organisation – or is intended to reach the general public.

Using an intranet

One way of restricting access to a website is to create an intranet. An intranet (note the spelling) is a closed system that has many of the features of the Internet but which is only accessible within an organisation.

An intranet is created on the organisation's own network system and can only be used by users who log on to stations on the network. It will normally include email services and an internal 'website'. Strictly speaking we should not really refer to the pages as a 'website' as it does not appear on the World Wide Web.

An intranet can hold confidential information that should not normally appear outside the organisation as well as day-to-day administrative arrangements. By definition, members of the public do not normally have access to intranets, but you may find that you have an intranet at your place of study.

Many employees travel around the country on business or work from home. They also need access to the company's intranet. The organisation may make it possible for them to access the intranet over an Internet connection, using an ID and password system to gain access. This is sometimes known as an extranet.

Maintenance and future development

A website should always be designed with maintenance in mind. A community site that is run by volunteers should not aim to update the site on a daily basis, as that is unlikely to be sustainable. So the site should be designed to look interesting without necessarily carrying immediate news.

On the other hand, an organisation that has ambitious plans for a site that will be updated several times a day, must ensure that enough staff are trained to provide material and to upload pages, and that fallback options are in place in case of staff absence.

Many large sites use content management systems, which allow non-technical staff to prepare web pages by simply copying text and images from elsewhere on their computers. These systems are often based on databases, which generate web pages automatically on demand, drawing on the data held in the database.

Information

Major websites are usually redesigned every year or two, to take advantage of the progress of technology and the addition of new features to browsers. If old material is still going to be accessible from the site, there is sometimes a problem around creating a new design that incorporates old material. The use of a database that holds the raw content can solve this problem because the page design is handled separately from the content.

→ Practise your skills 1

Use your usual search engine to find other e-commerce websites. Can you work out which kinds of business have gone in for e-commerce? And what kinds of business are rarely to be found on the Internet?

→ Check your knowledge

1 What is user-centred design?
2 List the stages in the design process.
3 What is e-commerce?
4 How can a target audience be described?
5 What is an intranet?

Designing a website

You will learn to

- Design websites for a target audience using storyboarding
- Create appropriate structure diagrams demonstrating the linking structure of web pages
- Produce project plans for the incremental development of websites, including the gathering of suitable resources
- Identify the importance of 'house style'
- Explain the relative merits of different page layout styles (standard, tables and frames)

Design specification

Based on the analysis, you should draw up a design specification which you then agree with your client. The design requirements of a website can be broken down into three areas: content, visual design, and technical design.

Content

The content of a site covers all the information that it will contain, together with any interactive features. All sites should normally include, as a minimum:

- How to contact the organisation – this information should always be provided somewhere on the site. This may be offered through an online form, or an email address may be given.
- Basic details about the organisation – who it includes and what it does.
- Privacy policy (if personal data is collected from the visitor) – this is a statement about how the organisation will handle any information given them by a visitor. This is necessary to comply with the Data Protection Act and to give the visitor the confidence to do business with the organisation.

In addition, the content part of the design specification should describe in outline:

- The information that should be provided – this should include text, visual information (charts, photographs, videos, etc.) and sound (music, etc.).
- The main categories of information – these will identify the headings that will appear in the main navigation bar.
- The style of language appropriate to the subject matter – business sites will tend to use more formal language than sites devoted to leisure interests; the age of expected visitors is also relevant.

As a general rule, visitors to your site should not be overwhelmed with information that they do not want. You can give links to more in depth coverage of a topic.

Note:

Navigation refers to the way a visitor finds their way around a website, using links provided on the pages. Text or images can act as navigation links, and image links are often called buttons. Some of the most important links may be positioned together in a navigation bar.

Visual design

The visual design of the site should specify:

- The overall impression – it could be businesslike, friendly, busy, formal, casual.
- Required components, such as company logo or corporate colours.
- Colour scheme – background, text and spot colours.
- Appearance of text – consistent text styles, length of paragraphs.
- Use of images – for information, as decoration, or to create a mood or style.
- Use of animation and video – appropriate use to entertain and inform.
- Layout of home page and of subsequent pages.

In general, a website should use all its visual elements consistently. The main navigation bar should be accessible throughout the site, and should appear in the same position on each page.

Technical design

The technical design concentrates on a number of usability issues:

- Navigation – links selected for main navigation bar, linking structure for all the other pages.
- Use of search tools – list boxes, keyword search boxes and site maps can help the visitor to find their way around.
- Download times – a web page should download within an acceptable time. The page itself as well as all the images on it have to be downloaded individually from the server, so altogether they should not usually take longer than one minute to download using the slowest communication link. Larger files can be made available provided the visitor is warned about their size.
- Browser compatibility – a web page can change in appearance when viewed with different browsers. The designer will try to minimise these variations.
- Maintenance – the site should be easy to maintain, that is, to update pages. The frequency of maintenance will depend on the purpose of the site.

Prototyping and implementation

A **prototype** is a cut-down version of the site which can be used as the basis for a design review with the client.

You create the first prototype, known as a **storyboard**, on paper to match the design specification. You usually sketch this by hand.

The storyboard should indicate:

- The layout of the home page and other pages.
- The links on the main navigation bar.
- The use of colour for background and text.
- The use of images for information and decoration.

The storyboard should be reviewed with the client. This discussion will often highlight aspects of the design specification that were overlooked or not specified clearly enough. At this stage, the client will often be inspired with new ideas for the site and these can also be incorporated into the design specification.

The designer next creates a **computer-based prototype**, based on the agreed storyboard, using web design software. The design is then subject to review and amendment, and this is repeated until the client is satisfied. The prototype will normally consist of the home page plus a small number of indicative pages.

Once the client has agreed on the prototype, the remaining pages can then be fully implemented.

Navigation

Navigation is the single most important usability aspect of a website. Your site is worthless if visitors cannot find their way around or cannot find specific information. There are several solutions to this.

Linking styles

Internal links allow the visitor to find their way around the site. Unless the site is very small you cannot provide links from any one page to all the other pages, so you have to design a navigation structure. You must consider how the pages are related to each other and work out what pages a visitor might want to see next.

Visitors can be divided into two types: those who are looking for specific information, and those who just want to look round. A site must provide links to suit both.

Linking by structure

Your website may naturally fall into a number of main sections, and in the main navigation bar you should give links to the first page in each section.

The structure of a website is often represented by the tree diagram that follows. A page is the **parent** to each of the pages below it in the structure, and is the **child** of any page above it. The child pages of the home page are particularly important, as they will always appear in the main navigation bar.

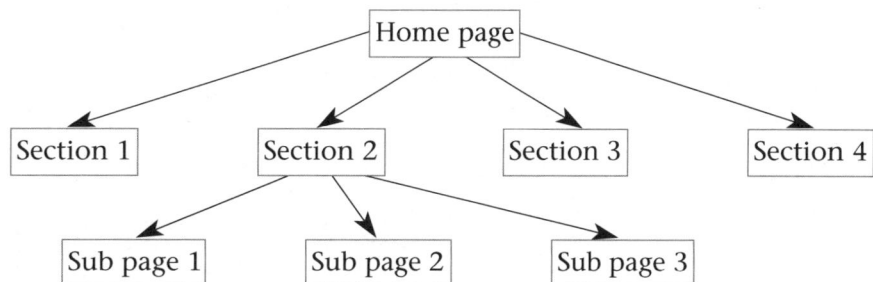

Case study – linking by structure at Tesco

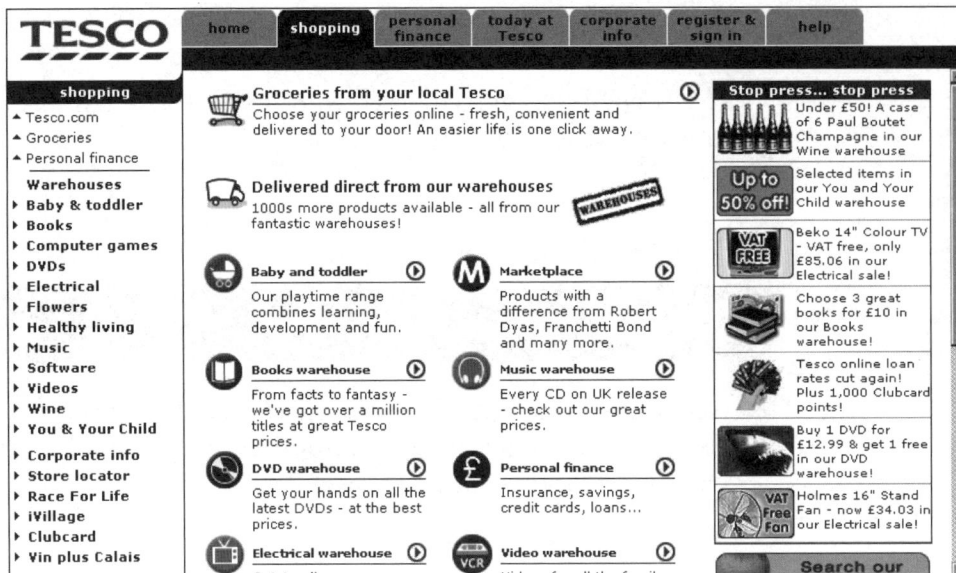

Figure 5.1 Linking by structure on Tesco's site

Tesco uses a strong structure to link its pages. The main navigation bar is shown as a series of tabs along the top of the screen and it appears on every page. The Shopping link has been selected and the first page of this section is displayed. A secondary navigation bar is on the left hand side of the screen and shows the links within the Shopping section. The secondary navigation bar is displayed on every page in the Shopping section.

Linking by theme

The Web allows visitors to browse to any page they like and in any order they like, so it is sometimes helpful if you provide links to other pages that cover similar topics. The diagram for this kind of linking will look like a random and rather messy network, as shown below. Linking by theme helps the visitor who just wants to surf.

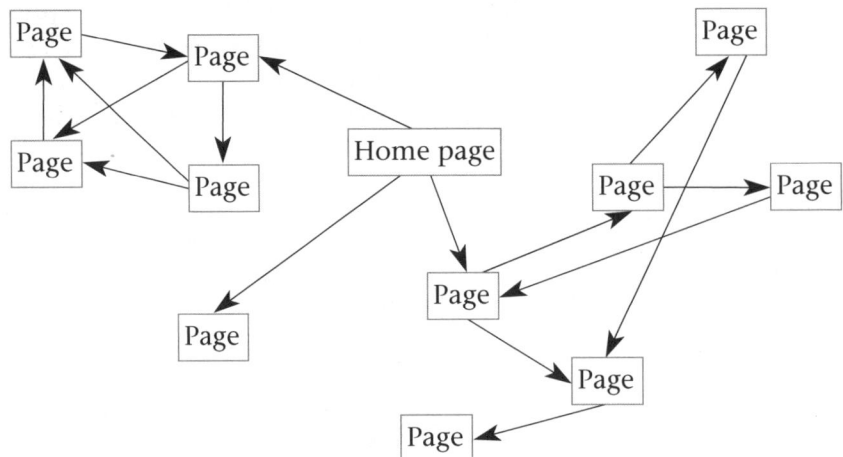

Combined linking styles

Many sites use a combination of linking by structure and linking by theme. Often, a selection from the main navigation bar on the home page leads to a page that holds both the main navigation bar and a secondary navigation bar. The page may also hold thematic links to other pages elsewhere on the site that contain content which may also be of interest to anyone who visits that page.

Case study – combining linking styles on a community site

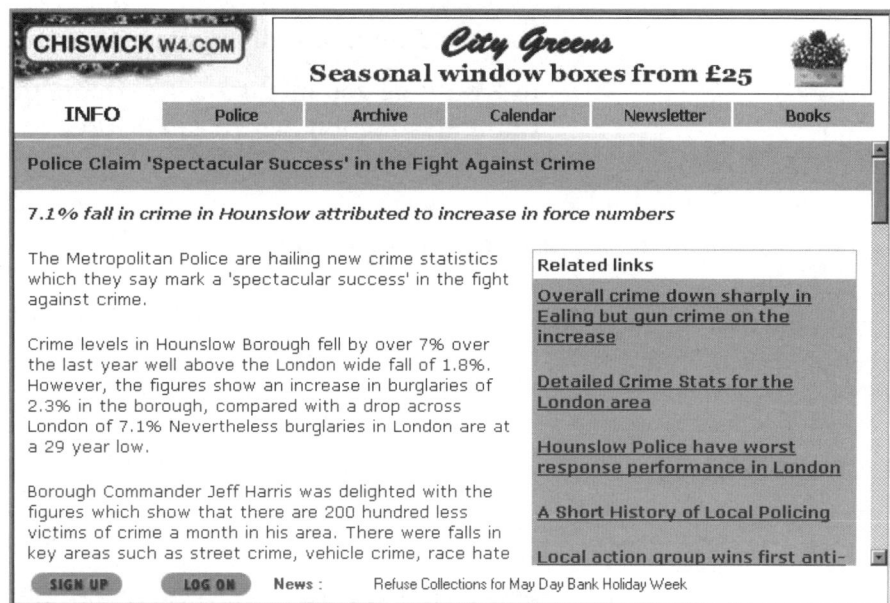

Figure 5.2 Linking by theme as well as by structure on a community site

The page shown is from a community site, which features news, events and comments about the local area. It has a main navigation bar along the top, but it also has some thematic links in the right-hand column. These link to other news stories about crime and policing.

Navigation bars

A navigation bar can be placed anywhere on a web page. The main navigation bar is often placed horizontally across the top of the page, or alternatively, vertically down the left side. If the main navigation bar is horizontal, then a secondary navigation bar can be placed immediately above or below it. Alternatively, it could be placed vertically.

If the main navigation bar is vertical it is quite difficult to place a secondary navigation bar alongside it. One solution to this problem is to use an expanding navigation bar. When an item is clicked a space opens up below the item revealing the secondary links.

Both horizontal and vertical navigation bars can be designed as menu-style navigation bars. When the mouse clicks or passes over the item a drop-down menu reveals the secondary links.

Indexes and site maps

A large site may need a handful of pages that contain little more than links to other pages. An index will list links to all the pages of a certain type. If the content of a site is managed by a database then these indexes may be generated automatically. A site map is an index listing every page on the site.

In FrontPage you might like to explore the facilities offered by the Table of Contents function, which can be used to generate both complete site maps and individual indexes.

Information

The 'three click rule' is a good guideline to follow. A visitor should be able to find any piece of information that they are seeking on a site with no more than three clicks of the mouse. This can be quite a challenge on a large site, but can be achieved with a combination of navigation bars, indexes and thematic links.

Page layouts

Websites should be designed to be viewable at all resolutions. At the time of writing over half of all users set their screens at a width of 1024 pixels or wider. Many commercial websites are still designed for 800 width resolution, to accommodate visitors using lower resolutions. Other sites are designed on the assumption that most users will have at least 1024 width resolution.

Standard (resizable) web pages

Standard web pages change their appearance, depending on the size of the browser window (Figure 5.3). These have the advantage of being viewable at all resolutions and with any window size. However, some web designers do not like working with resizable web pages as they cannot control the final appearance of the pages.

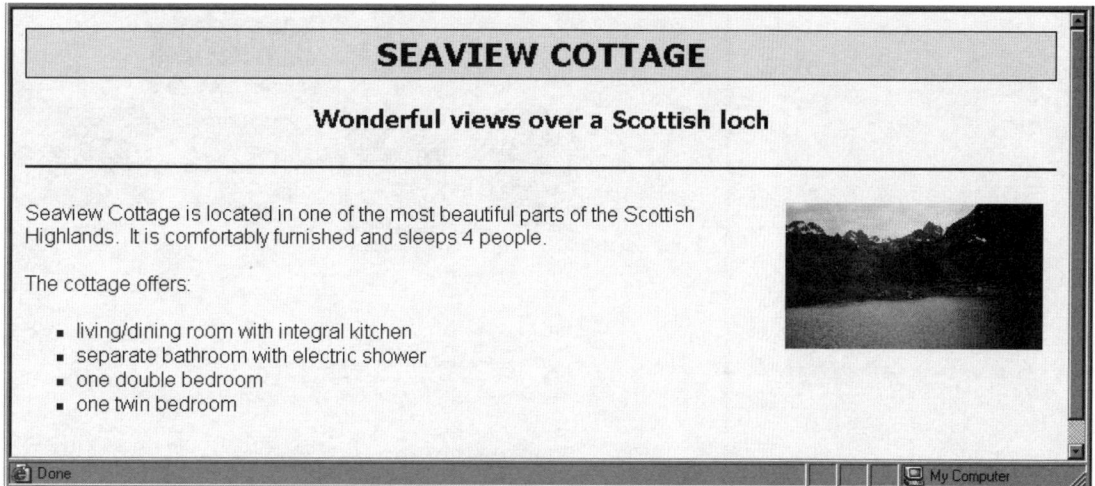

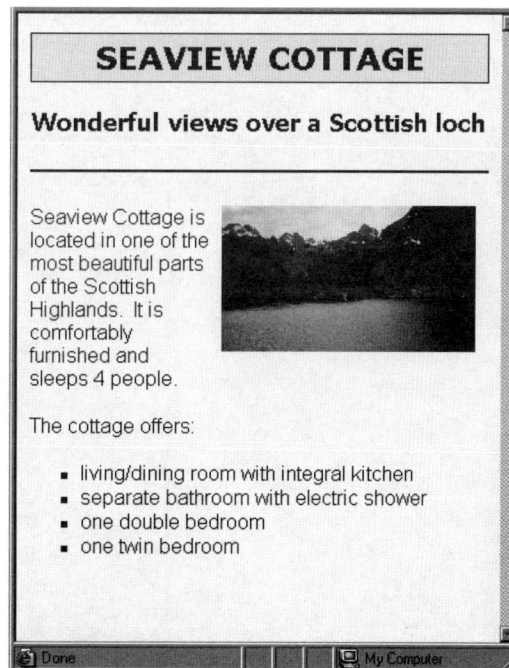

SEAVIEW COTTAGE

Wonderful views over a Scottish loch

Seaview Cottage is located in one of the most beautiful parts of the Scottish Highlands. It is comfortably furnished and sleeps 4 people.

The cottage offers:

- living/dining room with integral kitchen
- separate bathroom with electric shower
- one double bedroom
- one twin bedroom

SEAVIEW COTTAGE

Wonderful views over a Scottish loch

Seaview Cottage is located in one of the most beautiful parts of the Scottish Highlands. It is comfortably furnished and sleeps 4 people.

The cottage offers:

- living/dining room with integral kitchen
- separate bathroom with electric shower
- one double bedroom
- one twin bedroom

Figure 5.3 A standard, resizable web page displayed in two window sizes

Fixed size web pages

Fixed size web pages do not resize when the window is changed (Figure 5.4). Some web designers like to control the layout and appearance of pages carefully, to impose a fixed size on the page. One disadvantage of this is that if the visitor reduces the width of the window too much, horizontal scrollbars may appear.

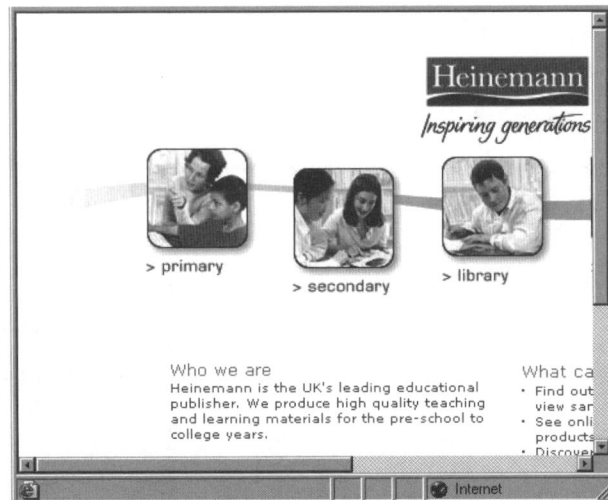

Figure 5.4 A fixed size web page displayed in two window sizes

Fixed size web pages can be achieved by using tables. The whole page is contained within a single table, which is fixed in size. The border of the table has to be set at zero, so that it is not visible on the web page.

More tables can then be placed within the page table to hold the text and graphics.

Frames

The display in a browser can be split into two or more frames, each of which holds a separate web page. This technique is often used so that constant information is shown in one frame while the contents of another frame may change. For example, a main navigation bar can be displayed in a narrow frame at the top or side of a page, with the main page contents varying according to which link has been selected.

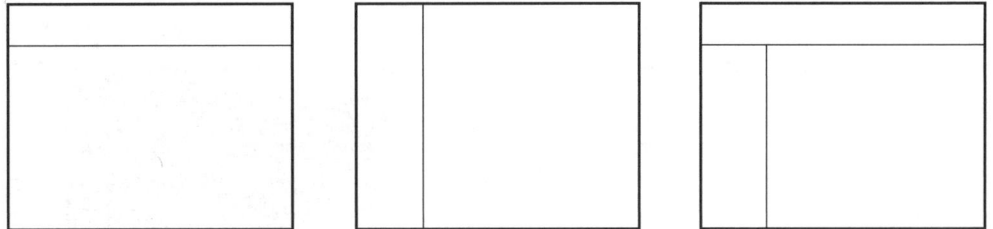

Figure 5.5 Three common frame configurations

The window in Figure 5.6 displays pages held inside two frames. On the left a narrow vertical frame holds the navigation bar that is used throughout the whole site. The main frame holds the page that has been selected. This page can be scrolled up and down while the frame on the page remains fixed in position, as shown in Figure 5.7.

When another page is selected from the navigation bar, only the contents of the main frame are changed (Figure 5.8).

Figure 5.6 Two frames in a window

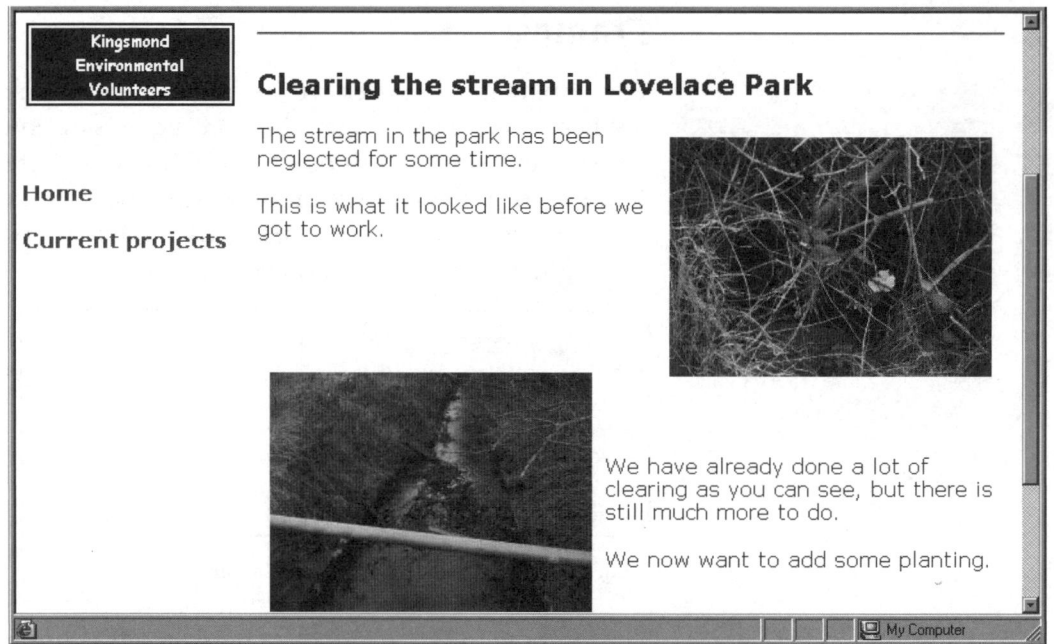

Figure 5.7 The page in the main frame scrolls past the side frame

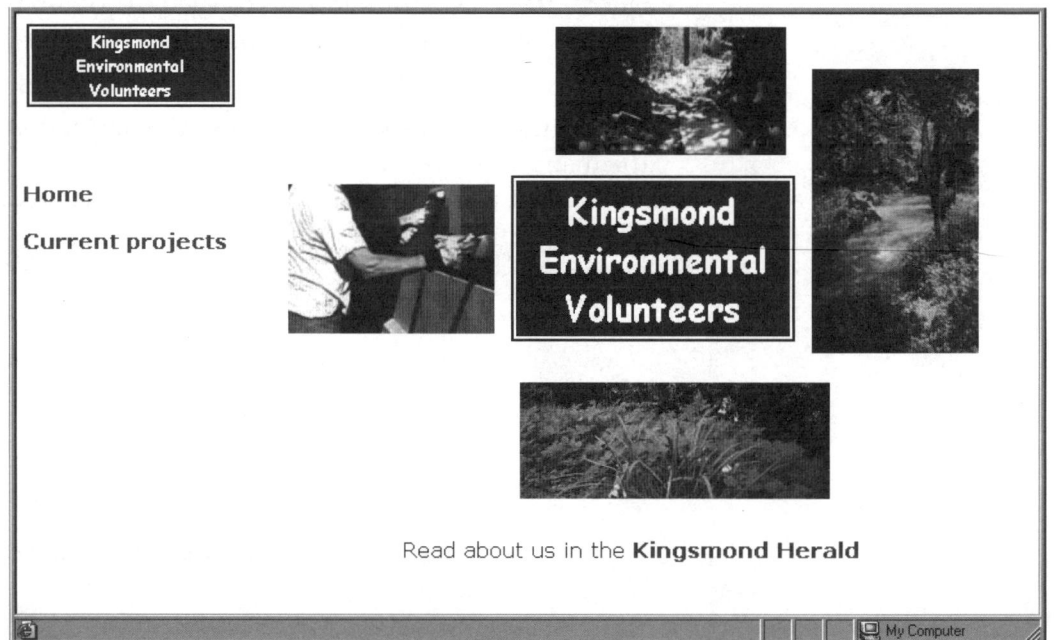

Figure 5.8 The contents of the side frame do not change when you select another page

A frame page is a separate web page that will not be visible to the visitor. Instead it describes the structure of the frames in the window and assigns initial pages to the frames. You can learn how to create frames in Section 11.

One disadvantage of using frames is that a search engine may link to only one of the pages. This means that the important information held in the pages which should be displayed alongside it may not be visible to the visitor.

House style

The house style of an organisation is a key factor in determining the visual design of a website. Most organisations have a style guide that lays down the correct use of company logos, and specifies the colours, fonts etc. to be used on all publications, including letters to the public. This ensures that the organisations' communications with the public have a consistent look and feel to them.

Most organisations want to carry their style guidelines through to their websites. This can usually be achieved although there are sometimes some constraints on the use of specific fonts or exact colour matching.

→ Practise your skills 1

Check other news sites, such as online newspapers or TV channels, to see whether they use a combination of linking by structure and linking by theme.

→ Practise your skills 2

1 Visit a number of websites and note down the linking styles that they use.
2 Draw a diagram to illustrate the linking on one or more of the sites. (You will only be able to do this for a site with relatively few pages.)
3 Check the types of page layouts used on the sites: standard (resizable), fixed size or with frames.

→ Practise your skills 3

1 Create a storyboard for a four page site on a subject of your choice. This site should not use frames.
2 The home page in your design will explain what the site is about. It will include at least two images.
3 One of the pages will display a photo gallery.
4 One of the pages will hold a mixture of text and graphics laid out neatly across and down the page.
5 One of the pages will have links at the top of the page to information further down. The information could be FAQs (Frequently Asked Questions), or simply sections in a long article.
6 Discuss your storyboard with others to gather further ideas and feedback.
7 You will use this storyboard in later sections, so keep it available.

→ Check your knowledge

1 What is the minimum information that should always be included on a business website?
2 What is a storyboard?
3 In the context of navigation styles, explain parent and child pages.
4 What is a navigation bar?
5 What is a frame?

Creating a complete website

You will learn to

- Use software to manage the development of websites
- Use hyperlinks to link to:
  - ☐ Pages within the same website
  - ☐ Other sites on the World Wide Web
  - ☐ Email
  - ☐ FTP (file transfer protocol)
- Create image maps
- Use metatags to add keyword information to pages that helps search engines

Site management software

A website consists of web pages that are linked together. You could create a number of single pages in a web authoring package and add the hyperlinks manually. A better approach is to use the website management tools that are built in to most web authoring packages. You can use these to automate many of the processes.

The site management tools in web authoring packages do vary, but they often enable the designer to:

- Manage the folders and files for a site.
- View and modify the navigation structure of a site.
- Create and maintain navigation bars automatically.
- Check all the hyperlinks.
- Create a site map.
- Create a design theme for a site.
- Publish the site to a server.
- Manage a website project.

Setting up a website

All websites include one page called index.htm or index.html. This is the first page that any visitor will download. When a URL, such as http://www.yahoo.com, is entered into the address box of a browser, the browser actually searches for the index page e.g. http://www.yahoo.com/index.htm. On many sites, the index page holds the home page, although it can sometimes hold instructions for downloading other pages.

> **Hint:**
>
> In FrontPage each website that you create is stored on your system in a separate web folder. FrontPage refers to these as webs. You can close a web folder by selecting **Close Web** from the **File** menu or by simply exiting from FrontPage. To open a web folder select **Open Web** from the **File** menu, and select the folder name.

Information

FrontPage provides a number of tools in the Views bar that help you construct and manage a site. To see how they work, use one of the website templates or wizards to create an instant site. You should not use these whole site templates for assessment work, but they are a quick way of demonstrating the principles.

Method

I   Select **File**, then **Close** to close any pages or webs that are open.

2   Select **File**, then **New**, then **Page or Web**. This opens the **Task Pane**. In the **Task Pane**, select **Website Templates**. In the Website Templates dialogue box select **Personal Web** (Figure 6.1). To the right you will see a text box in which you can specify the location of a new web. The default location for all FrontPage webs is in a folder called My Webs. Change the default name of the folder to 'personal'. FrontPage will create the folder for you.

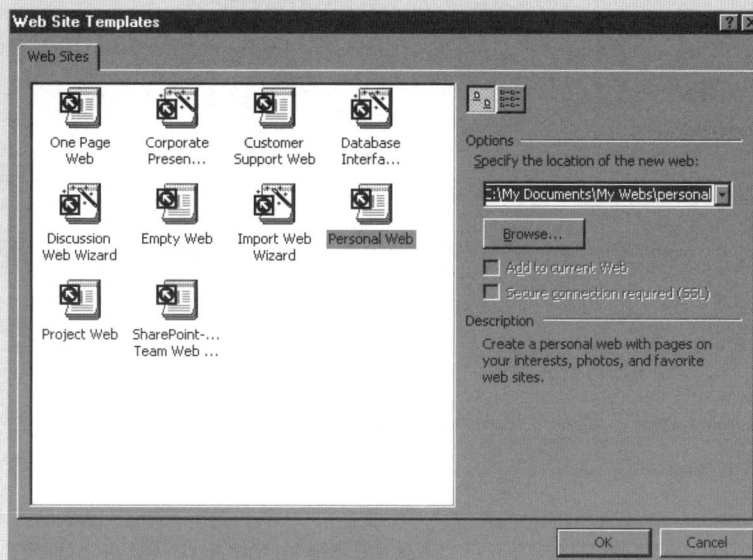

Figure 6.1 Setting up a new web in FrontPage

3   **Folders.** Click on the **Folders** icon in the **Views** bar. FrontPage has created a new web folder and generated six web pages in the personal website. It has also created private and images folders specifically for this website.

4   Double-click on index.htm, then view the page in Preview mode. You can now explore the website, which is not, of course, finished, but do not edit the pages. Close any open pages before the next steps.

5   **Reports**. The Reports view on the **Views** bar lists some statistics about the site which will become more significant as your site grows.

6   **Navigation.** You can see how all the pages are linked together by selecting the Navigation view (Figure 6.2). You can edit any page by clicking on it in Navigation view, and this is usually the most convenient way of accessing pages. The Navigation view can be used to add new pages to your website structure.

Figure 6.2 The navigation structure of a personal website in FrontPage

7 **Hyperlinks.** The Hyperlinks view displays links between pages. Click on the index page to view its links (Figure 6.3). Note the direction of the arrows in the diagram – on the left end of an arrow is the page which carries the hyperlink and on the right end is the page or external website that it links to. Click on the + buttons to expand the diagram.

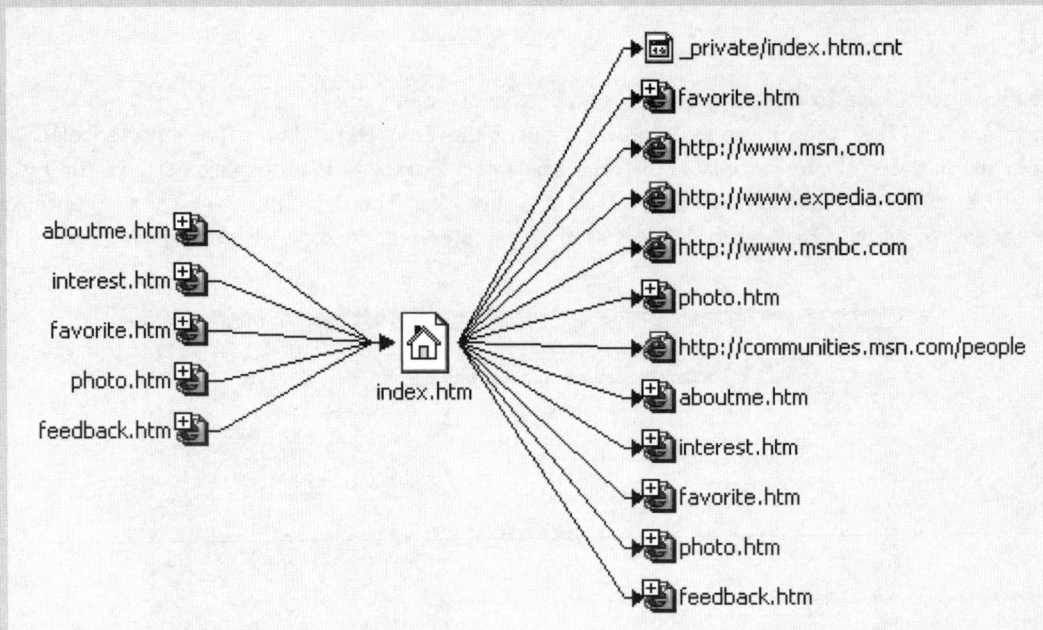

Figure 6.3 Hyperlinks view of a website in FrontPage

8 **Tasks.** This view allows you to list all the tasks that you have to complete and is a very useful planning tool.

Task 6.2	Creating a complete web using site management tools

For this task, you will create a web for a fast food outlet in FrontPage. The home page will give basic information, such as the name, address, phone number, and details about the delivery service. A second page will contain the fast food menu, and another page will list any job vacancies in the company.

Method

1 Close any open webs and select **File**, **New**, then **Page or Web**. In the Task Pane select **Website Templates**. Create a new **One Page Web**, and specify its location in a folder called 'megafood'.

2 Click on **Folders** in the **Views** bar. The index (home) page has been created for you. Double-click on the index page and it will open in Page view.

3 Simply enter the name and address and any other text, as in Figure 6.4. Save the page.

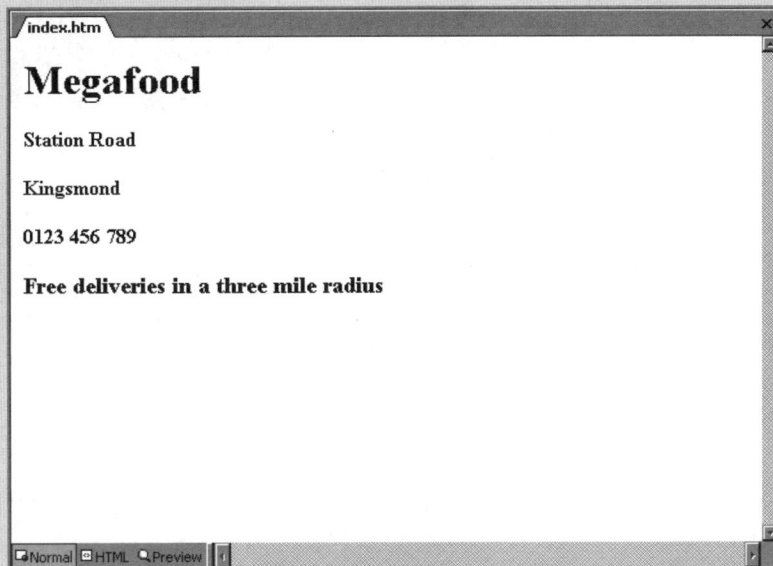

Figure 6.4 An index page for a site for a fast food business

4   Select **File**, **New**, then **Page or Web**. In the **Task Pane** select **Blank Page**. Create a new page and save it as menu.htm. You can use a table to hold the menu as in Figure 6.5.

5   Create another page and save it as jobs.htm.

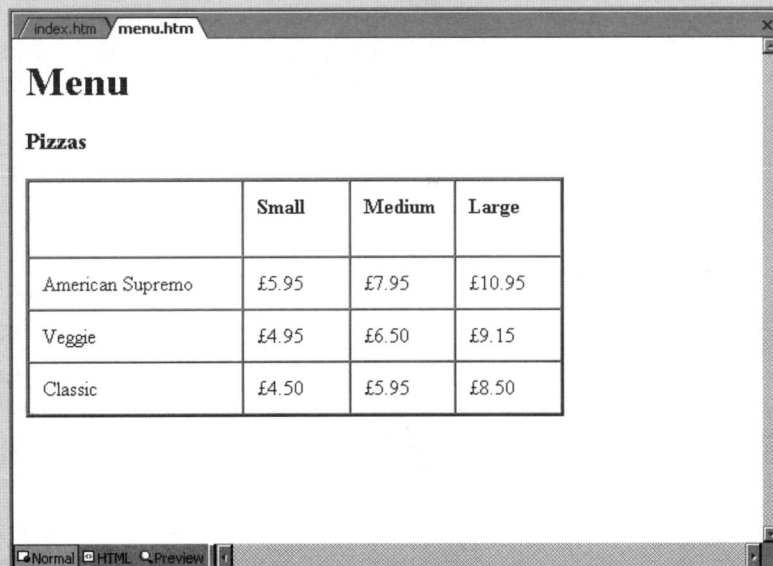

Figure 6.5 The folder list in FrontPage and a basic page

Hint:

It is a good idea to set up the site and sort out the navigation before defining the styles.

Using site management tools to create navigation bars

Site management tools usually assume that the site has a tree structure. They can sometimes generate and insert one or more navigation bars to a page on demand. Any additional links must be created individually on the page.

Method

1. Open the fast food site, or if it is already open, close any pages.
2. Click on the **Navigation** view.
3. An icon representing the index page will be shown, as in Figure 6.6, with the title 'Home Page'

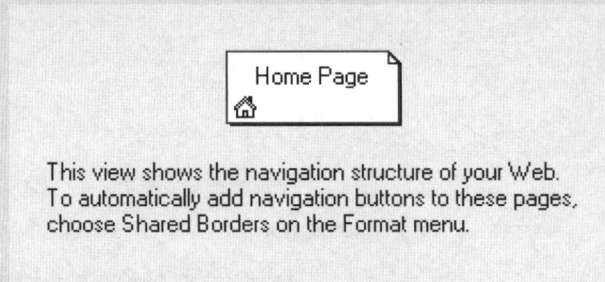

Figure 6.6 The index page for the fast food website displayed in Navigation view in FrontPage

4. If the Folder List is not displayed, click on the **Toggle Pane** button.
5. Drag the menu and jobs pages from the Folders list on to the diagram to give the navigation structure as shown in Figure 6.7. This has defined the relationships between the pages.

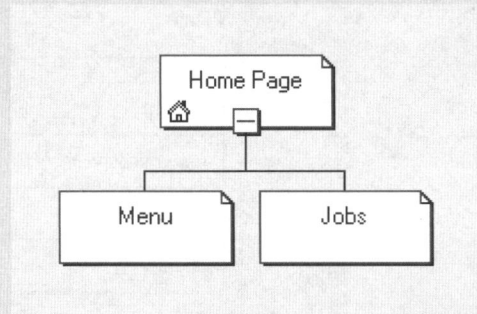

Figure 6.7 The navigation structure in FrontPage for the fast food website

Information

In Figure 6.7 the index page (home page) is the **parent** to the menu and jobs pages, and the menu and jobs pages are both a **child** of the index page.

6   The site management tools can now create the navigation bars on the pages. Open the index page by double-clicking on its name in the Folders list or on the page icon in Navigation view. Place the cursor where you want the navigation bar to appear. Select **Insert**, then **Navigation**.

7   Under 'Choose a bar type', select **Bar based on navigation structure**. On the next page select **Use Page's Theme**. On the next page select the image showing horizontal links. Click **Finish**. In the Link Bar Properties dialogue box select Child level (Figure 6.8).

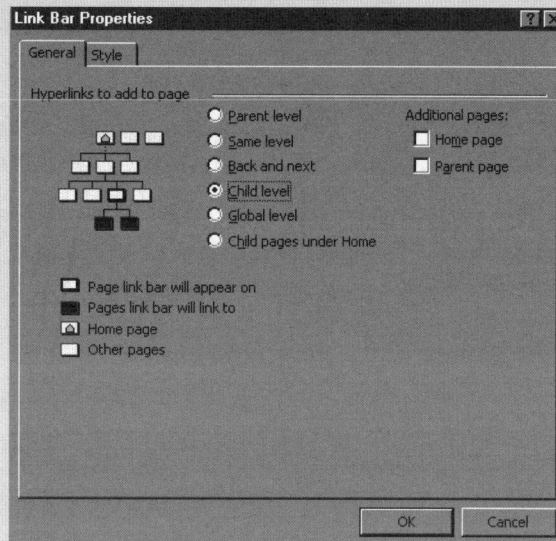

Figure 6.8 Setting the properties of a navigation bar in FrontPage

8   In Preview mode the page should look similar to Figure 6.9. The buttons do not look very impressive, but can be transformed by the use of style sheets or themes.

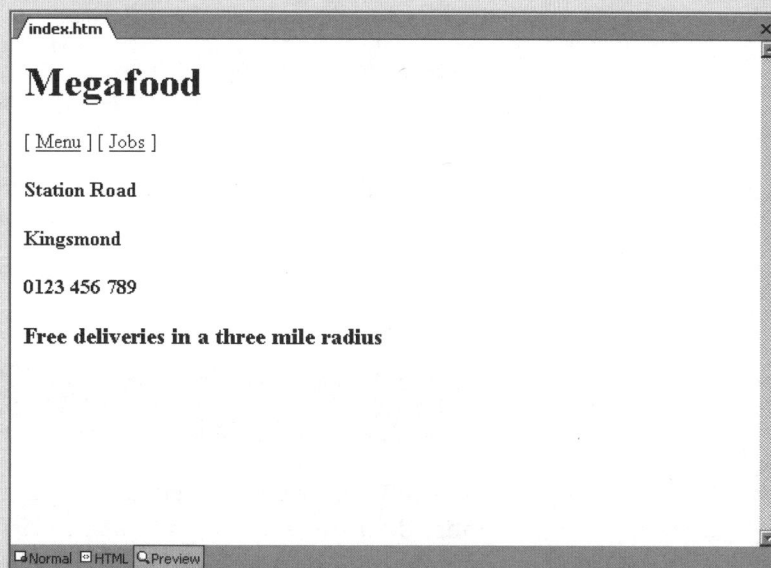

Figure 6.9 A navigation bar created on the index page by FrontPage

9   You now need to add navigation bars to the other two pages. Repeat the process that you used for the home page. In the Link Bar Properties dialogue box provide links to pages at the same level, and also to the Home page (as an additional page).

10   When you try out the links in Preview mode you will see that the navigation bar includes a non-functioning button that refers to the page that it is on (Figure 6.10). This is equivalent to a greyed-out item on a drop-down menu in Windows-based software. It is important to include this non-functioning button as it means that the navigation bar items appear in the same positions on different pages. FrontPage always places the Home button to the left of the others.

11   Save all the changes that you have made.

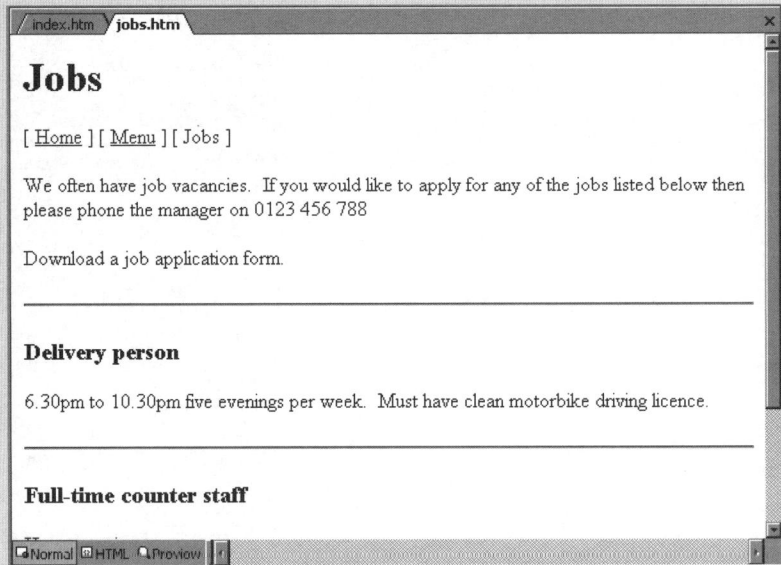

Figure 6.10 The Jobs page with a navigation bar created in FrontPage

The Navigation bar tool in FrontPage generates HTML something like this at the position where the navigation bar is inserted:

```
<!--webbot bot="Navigation" S-Type="children" S-Orientation=
"horizontal" S-Rendering="graphics" B-Include-Home B-Include-
Up U-Page S-Target -->
```

This is not standard HTML code, but calls on a procedure – a webbot – that is specific to FrontPage. The Navigation bar tool can create text or image hyperlinks.

Use hyperlinks

On the Web, the links between pages create one vast global network. An individual site will ensure that the visitor explores what the site has to offer by offering internal links to other pages on the same site, as well as external links to other sites.

All web authoring packages allow you to convert text or an image into a hyperlink. In FrontPage the Insert menu includes a Hyperlink item which opens up a dialogue box.

In HTML the tag used for a hyperlink is <a> , where <a> stands for 'anchor'. The code for a link to a page called news.htm looks like this:

```
<a href="news.htm">Latest news</a>
```

> **Information**
>
> - **href**, standing for hyperlink reference, states the location that the hyperlink links to.

An image can be used as a button instead of text for a hyperlink. The code will look like this:

```
<a href="news.htm"><img border="0" src="images/newsbutton.gif"
width="120" height="30"> Latest news</a>
```

Task 6.4 — Adding other hyperlinks

> **Method**
>
> 1 Open the fast food site.
> 2 First, create an external hyperlink. Add text on one of the pages to link to an external site (example of Megafood International given in Figure 6.11). Highlight the text and select **Hyperlink** from the **Insert** menu.
> 3 In the **Address** box, enter the full URL of the website, including http://
> 4 Alternatively, click on the Browse the Web icon, and find the correct page with your browser. When you switch back to FrontPage the URL will be entered in the box.

Hyperlinks to other sites

A hyperlink can also link to a page in another website. In that case the full URL must be given:

```
<a href="http://news.bbc.co.uk/" target="_blank">BBC News</a>
```

> **Information**
>
> - **target** defines the window where the page is opened. The default value is the same page; target="_blank" opens the page in a new window.

Links to other sites can be added to any web page. Some sites provide no external links at all, because they do not want the visitor to leave the site once there. On the other hand, some sites contain many links to other sites, and where that is their main purpose they are known as **portal sites**.

Other uses of hyperlinks

A hyperlink can also be used to send an email:

```
<a href="mailto://myname@thisismydomain.co.uk" >Email me</a>
```

When this hyperlink is clicked, a new email window opens in the visitor's email client software, with the email address in the recipient field.

You can also create a hyperlink that will allow the visitor to download a file from the site. This can be any sort of file – word processing file, program file etc. The file can be transferred using either HyperText Transfer Protocol (HTTP) or File Transfer Protocol (FTP). The HTML in each case would look like:

```
<a href="http://thisismydomain.co.uk/mydocument.doc">Download
the document</a>
```

```
<a href="ftp://thisismydomain.co.uk/mydocument.doc">Download
the document</a>
```

Task 6.5   Adding an email link

Method

1	Open the fast food site.
2	Enter text inviting people to email the manager. Highlight the text, and then select **Hyperlink** from the **Insert** menu.
3	Click on Email address. Type in an email address.
4	Use Preview mode to check that these links work correctly before saving the changes.

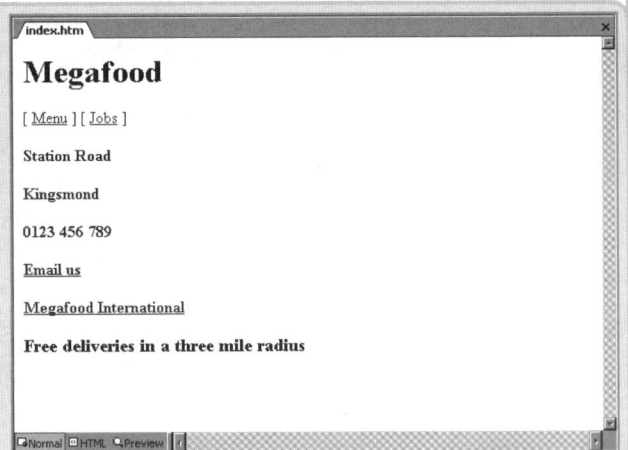

Figure 6.11 External and email hyperlinks

Checking the web pages in a browser

You should check the pages you have created from time to time in a browser. In FrontPage use Preview in Browser from the File menu. The most important reason for doing this is to check that the links work correctly. But you can also use see how the pages fit into different sized windows and how the site looks in different browsers.

Create image maps

You can create hotspots on an image. A hotspot is an area of an image that acts as a hyperlink and an image that has hotspots on it is known as an image map. Image maps can be used as highly graphical navigation bars. They can also be used to help the viewer identify items on a plan or geographical map of an area.

Web authoring packages usually provide an image mapping tool that you can use to develop them. They are a bit tricky to create directly in HTML, but again image mapping tools are available for HTML editors.

You are going to create a map of an area which will show the delivery area for Megafood. This will be placed on the home page.

Method

1   First create an imaginary map in a painting package. Alternatively, you could download a map from a website to experiment with.

2   Open the fast food site. Insert the map on the home page.

3   Click on the image and the Picture toolbar will appear. In the Picture bar there are four hotspot buttons ▭ ⬭ ⌐ ⬚ .

4   Click on the **Circular Hotspot** button. On the map, draw a circle centred on the shop location as shown in Figure 6.12.

5   When you lift up the mouse button the **Insert Hyperlink** dialogue box appears. From the list click on the **Menu** page and click OK. If you cannot see the page, click on **Existing File or Web Page.**

6   You can now create hotspots for the areas outside the shop delivery zone. These could link to the websites of other shops, or to a new page that lists other shops.

7   Click on the Preview mode to check that it works correctly.

8   When you save the page you will be reminded to save the map in the images folder. Click OK.

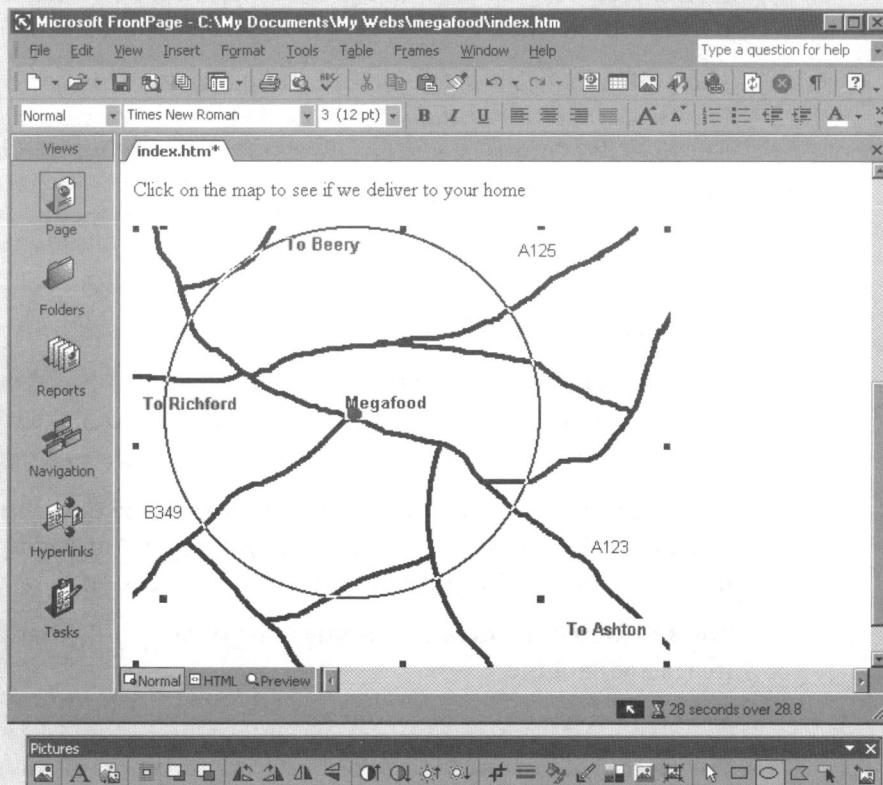

Figure 6.12 Outlining the area with the Circular Hotspot button

Complete your site

Adding visual design elements

So far your site does not use any text styles or other design features. As we saw in Section 2, the best option for a professional looking site is to use style sheets. These will be explored in more detail in the next section.

Using metatags and other head tags

The HTML code between the <head> tags of a page, such as those below, contains some important information.

```
<head>
<meta http-equiv="Content-Type" content="text/html;
charset=windows-1252">
<meta name="GENERATOR" content="Microsoft FrontPage 5.0">
<meta name="ProgId" content="FrontPage.Editor.Document">
<title>Menu</title>
</head>
```

These tags provide information about the page that follows, and a number of them are used by search engines. These can be edited directly in the HTML code, or web authoring tools can be used instead.

The **<title> tag** gives the title of the page, and this has two important functions. The title usually appears in the browser title bar. Web authoring packages like FrontPage often use the first line of text on the page for the title, but it can be changed to something like:

```
<title>Pizzas, pastas and more to enjoy at Megafood</title>
```

> ### Information
>
> Search engines display the title of a page when they list a site in response to a query, so that is a good reason to make it meaningful.

The remaining tags are known as **metatags**. The default ones created by the web authoring package should not be changed, but a couple of very important ones are omitted and should be added in.

The **keyword metatag** contains a list of keywords that people might use in a search engine.

```
<meta name="keywords" content="Megafood, fast food, pizza, pasta">
```

The **description metatag** contains a description of the site which may also be quoted by a search engine when it lists a site.

```
<meta name="description" content="Welcome to Megafood – where you
can find the best fast food in Kingsmond. Pizzas, pastas and more.">
```

→ Practise your skills 1

1   In FrontPage set up a new web for a small garden centre. The home page will give a general introduction to the centre, with address and contact details. It will link to three other pages containing information – one about plants, one about garden furniture and one about garden products such as tools and fertilisers.

2   Add some basic information on each page – you can add more detail later.

3   Set up the navigation structure for the site.

4   Create navigation bars on each page.

5   Add an email link to the home page.

6   Add at least one link to an external website.

7   Enhance the site by, for example, adding images, using a table to display products, using a FrontPage theme etc.

→ Practise your skills 2

1   In FrontPage set up a new web for a family medical information website.

2   The home page will hold an image map which provides the main navigation to the other pages. The image map will be a picture of a person. When the visitor clicks on a part of the body it will link to a page about that part.

3   Create two pages of information, each about a specific part of the body, e.g. feet, ears, eyes.

4   In Microsoft Paint, create a simple image of a person. Alternatively you can find a suitable web image from an Internet site.

5   Insert the image on the home page.

6   Create an image map. Try out the four hotspot buttons to see which one is most useful for this task. Create hotspots on the image to act as links to the pages you have created.

7   Add suitable metatags to the pages.

8   Enhance the site in any way you like.

→ Check your knowledge

1   What is the index page of a website?

2   What can you use hyperlinks for, apart from linking to another page or another website?

3   What are metatags and why is it important to include them?

Cascading style sheets and page templates

You will learn to

- Create templates for pages used within a website based upon house styles

Create style templates

Well designed sites have a consistent look, with the same textual and graphical elements repeated across all the pages.

In creating a consistent design the following design components should be considered:

- Font type, size, style and colour.
- Background colours and images for page, table and cells.
- Graphic elements such as lines, buttons and images.

The implementation of the visual design can be approached using three distinct methods – text formatting, themes (provided by web authoring packages) and style sheets. Of these, style sheets are by far the most flexible. They can also be created in any web development environment, whether you are working directly with HTML or using a full web authoring package.

Style sheets are particularly important for sites that have been designed in a specific house style. The pre-set themes that can be found in web authoring packages are not suitable. The style sheet should be set up at the beginning of the process, not added in later.

Using Cascading Style Sheets (CSS)

You have already created an embedded style sheet in Section 2. This contained the style definitions between the <head> and </head> tags. This method is suitable for styles that apply to one page only.

When you create a full site you will want to apply the same styles consistently across all the pages. To do this, the best approach is to create an external style sheet document that is then used by all the pages.

A style sheet is a separate page, hidden from the visitor, which is uploaded to the server along with the web pages. It contains a set of definitions for the styles used in the style list. In fact, any tag in the HTML code can have its own style definition.

The style definitions in a style sheet can be applied to all the pages on a site. That means that a simple change to the style sheet can have an affect right across a large site, and in this way visual consistency can be maintained.

A style sheet can be created in a web authoring package or in any text editor, such as Notepad. Sample style sheets are often provided as well, and these can be a good starting point.

External style sheets are referred to as Cascading Style Sheets, and carry the file extension .css

Task 7.1	Set up a web and create an external style sheet

Method

1 In FrontPage, close any open webs, select **File**, **New**, then **Page or Web**, then select **Empty Web** from the Task Pane.
2 Specify the name of the web in the Options box – in this example we have used 'sportsclub' as the name. Then click on OK.
3 Select **Folders** in the **Views** bar (Figure 7.1).

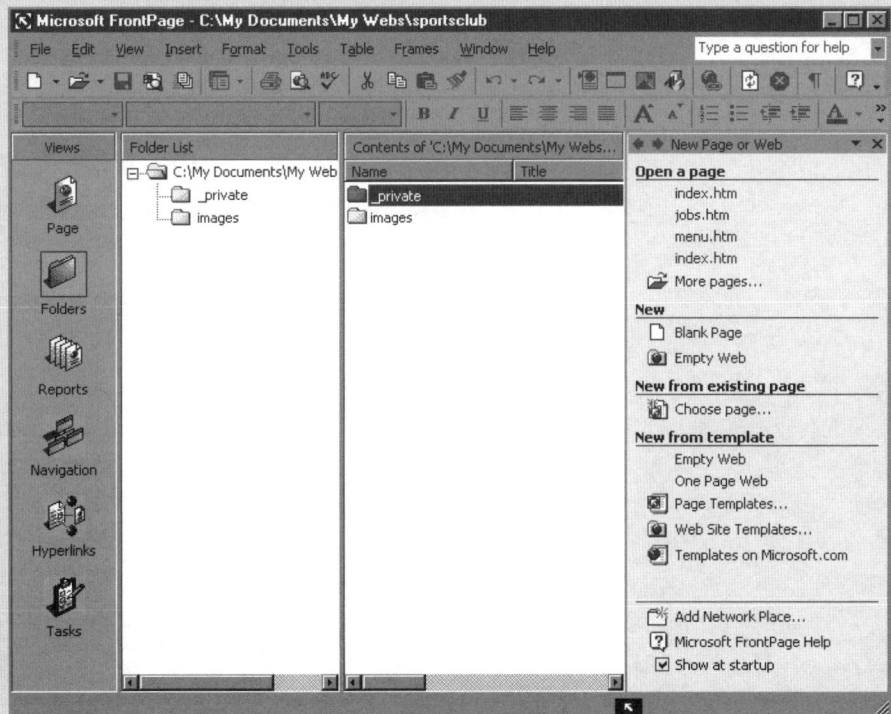

Figure 7.1 A new empty web

4 You will start by creating a style sheet. In the **Task Pane**, select **Page Templates**. Click on the style sheets tab. Select one of the predesigned style sheets, such as 'Capsules' (Figure 7.2).

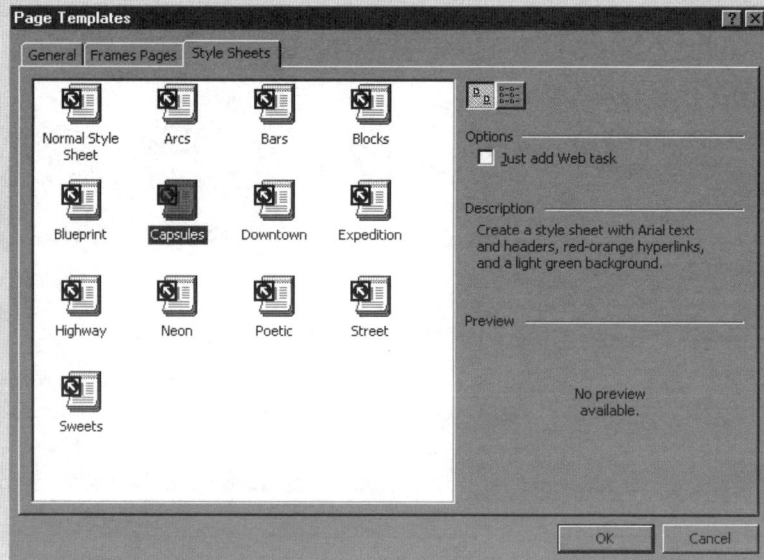

Figure 7.2 Selecting a pre-designed style sheet

5 The style sheet code appears with a floating toolbar. Have a look at the style definitions, but don't change them for now.

6 Save the style sheet as styles.css (Figure 7.3).

```
a:link
{
    color: rgb(255,102,51);
}
a:visited
{
    color: rgb(0,204,204);
}
a:active
{
    color: rgb(204,153,51);
}
body
{
    font-family: Arial, Helvetica;
    background-color: rgb(204,255,204);
    color: rgb(0,0,0);
}
table
{
    table-border-color-light: rgb(153,204,153);
    table-border-color-dark: rgb(153,204,153);
}
h1, h2, h3, h4, h5, h6
{
    font-family: Arial, Helvetica;
}
```

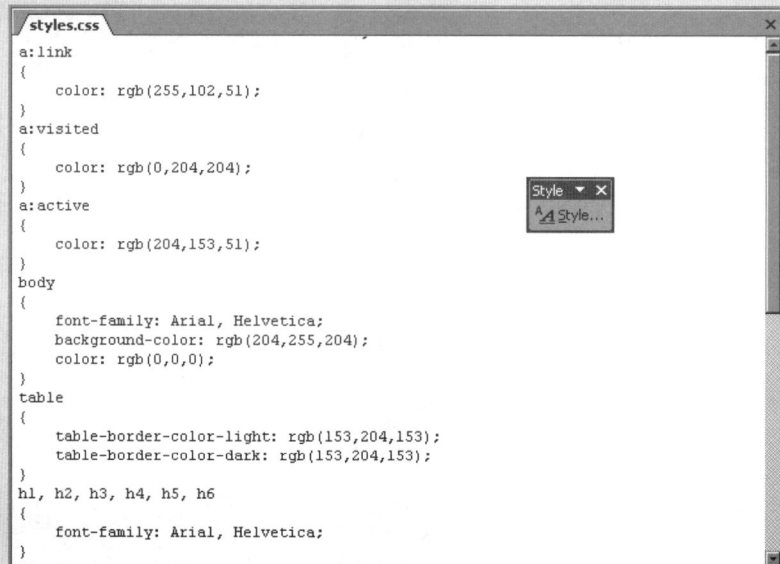

Figure 7.3 A style sheet

Creating a template

A template is a pre-designed page that can be used as the basis for all the pages in a web. Web authoring packages provide you with a number of templates that you can use, but you can also create your own. These are all stored in a system file and are displayed whenever you create a new page.

Information

If you are working in a HTML editor then you can simply create a page linked to a style sheet, and save it with a name like mytemplate.htm

---

Task 7.2	Create a template

Method

1 In the same web that you used in Task 7.1, you can now create a template that you will use for all the pages in the web.

2 Start by creating a blank new page. Select **File**, **New**, then **Page or Web**. Select **Page Templates** and click on **Normal Page**. This is the standard page template. You are going to adapt it and then save your own template for this web.

3 On the blank page, type in some basic indicative text. Apply the Heading styles from the style list. Then add any text that will appear on every page in the web.

4 Now save this page as a template. Select **Save As** from the **File** menu. In the Save As dialogue box, select **FrontPage Template** (*.tem) in the Save As Type box. Click on **Save**.

5 In the Save As Template dialogue box (Figure 7.5), The Title will be the name of the template as it will appear in the New Page dialogue box. The Name is the actual filename (FrontPage will add the correct filename extension). The Description will also appear in the Page Templates dialogue box (see Figure 7.8).

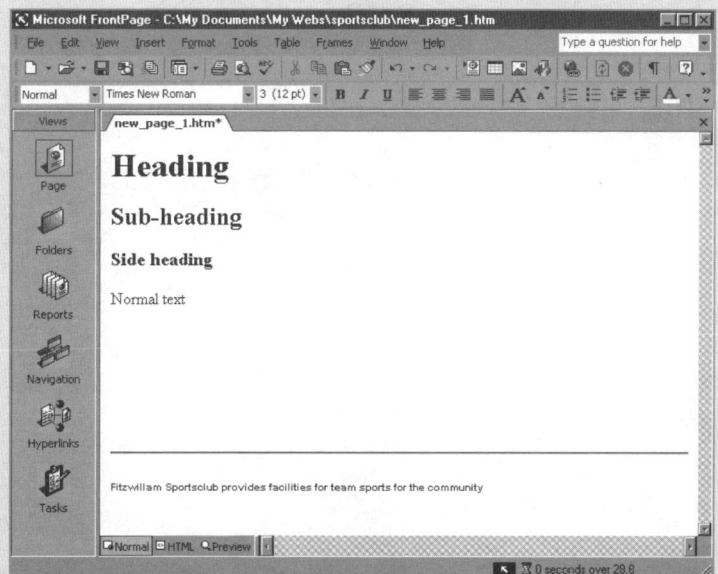

Figure 7.4 Setting up a template

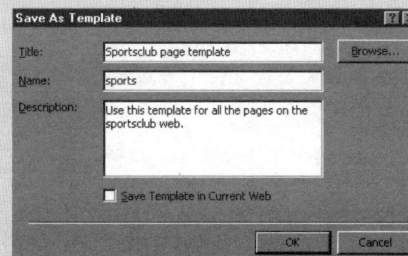

Figure 7.5 The Save As Template dialogue box

6 You now need to create a link to the style sheet from this page. Select **Style Sheet Links** in the **Format** menu. Click on **Add**, then click on styles.css in the file list. Click OK. Back in the **Link Style Sheet** dialogue box, click on styles.css as in Figure 7.6, then click on OK.

7 Click on the Save button to save the template linked to the style sheet. Close the template.

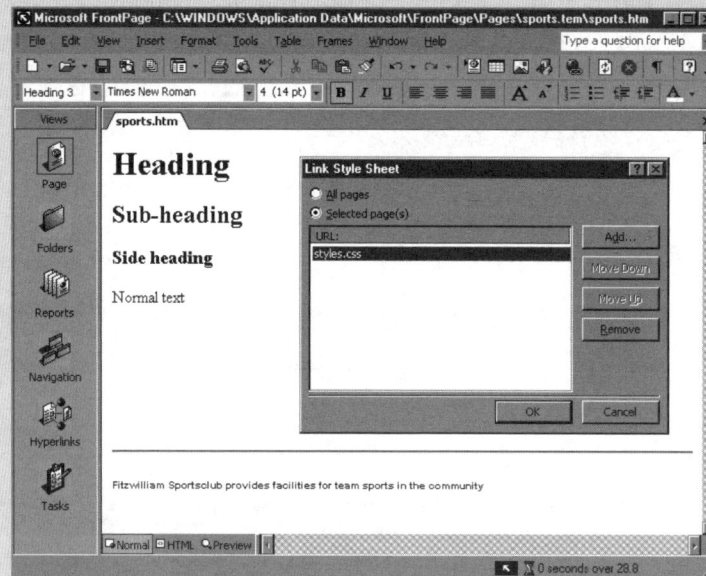

Figure 7.6 Linking a style sheet to a page

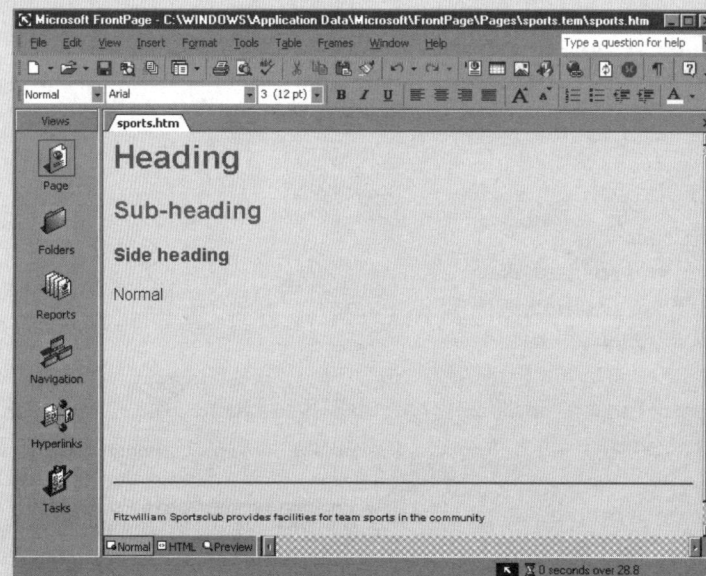

Figure 7.7 The effect of using the Capsules style sheet with the template

Using a template

Method

1   In the same web as before, select **File**, **New**, then **Page or Web**. Select **Page Templates**. You should now see the template among the pre-designed ones (Figure 7.8).
2   Select this template. You now have a new page based on the template. This will be the home page for the web. Add suitable text and save this as index.htm
3   Choose the template whenever you want to add a new page to the web.

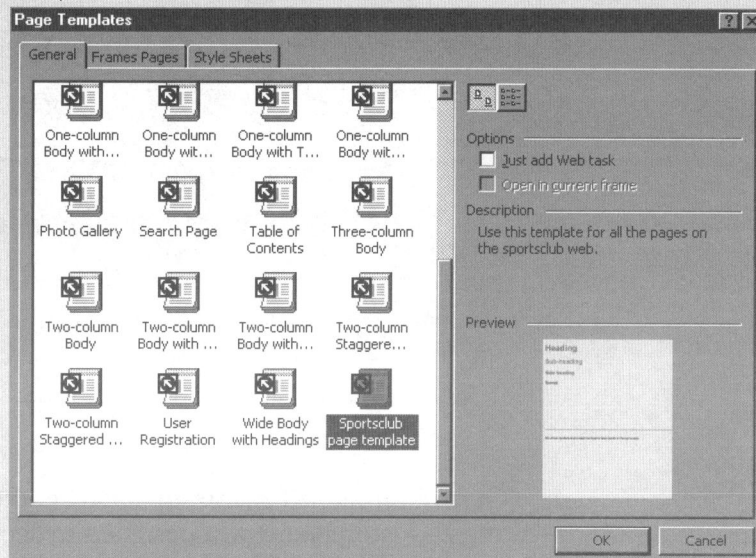

Figure 7.8 Using a template that you have created

Hint:

The template you have created in FrontPage will appear along with the pre-designed ones. Whenever you want to add a new page to your website, you should use this template.

Modifying the style sheet

If you check the HTML for a page created with a template, you will find this line inserted within the head of the page:

```
<link rel="stylesheet" type="text/css" href="styles.css">
```

You can make changes to the style sheet at any time. You will not have to change the template as it is permanently linked to the style sheet.

Task 7.4 Change a style sheet

Method

1   Open the same web used in Task 7.3, and open styles.css
2   Click on the **Styles** button in the Styles floating toolbar. You can now modify any of the styles in the style sheet. You can also add a new style definition from the list of HTML tags.
3   You will notice three tags called a:link, a:visited and a:active. These format hyperlinks. Do not change them as you will meet them again later.

4 Save the modified style sheet.

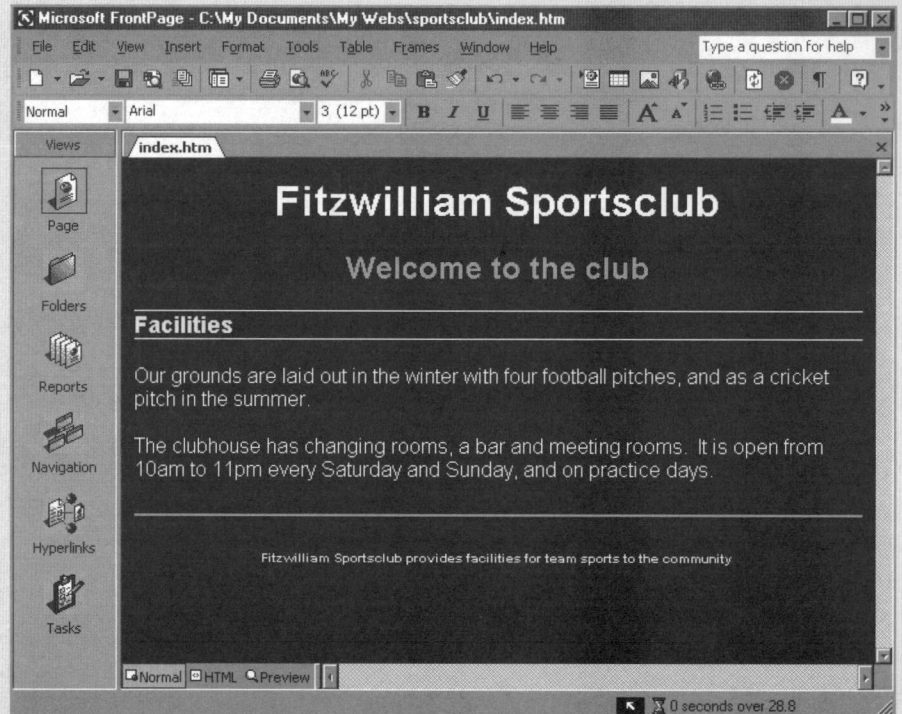

Figure 7.9 A page based on a template and a modified style sheet

→ Practise your skills 1

1 In FrontPage set up a new empty web. This should be based on the storyboard you designed in Section 5 (Practise your skills 3).

2 Create a style sheet using one of the pre-designed style sheets, and save it.

3 Set up a template by creating a new page. Add standard headings.

4 Link the new page to the style sheet.

5 Save the new page as a template.

6 Create a new blank page for the web using the template. This will be the home page. Save it as index.htm

7 Add text to the page, using the styles from the style list.

8 Open the style sheet and make changes to it to create an overall design for your web.

9 Check the appearance of the page you have created.

10 Save this web – you will continue to work on it in later sections.

→ Check your knowledge

1 What is a template?

2 What is the difference between an embedded style sheet and an external style sheet?

Section 8

Use web authoring software to manipulate images on web pages

You will learn to

- Resize images within websites:
  - ☐ For use as background images on pages
  - ☐ For use as icons or thumbnails
  - ☐ To specific dimensions
- Embed images within web pages
  - ☐ Set suitable alignment attributes
  - ☐ Use the Alt tag to provide the user with alternative meaningful information
- Apply transparency to images
- Describe the advantage of 'transparency' when applied to an image

Embed images

Images viewed on web pages are stored as independent files. This means that when a page is downloaded into a browser, the browser then has to download each of the image files from the server as well. So all the image files that are used on a web page are stored on the server alongside the page files.

It is common practice to store all the images on a website in a folder called 'images'. A web authoring package always provides a means of inserting images on a page, usually from an Insert menu.

Information

This task assumes that you already have an image that is the right size and file format for the page.

Task 8.1 Adding an image

Method

1 Open the sportsclub web that you created earlier.
2 In FrontPage, in Normal mode, place the cursor at the point where you want an image to appear, then select **Insert**, **Picture**, then **From File**. You will have to click on the folder icon in the dialogue box in order to navigate to the location where the image is stored on your system. The image should appear on the page, as in Figure 8.1.

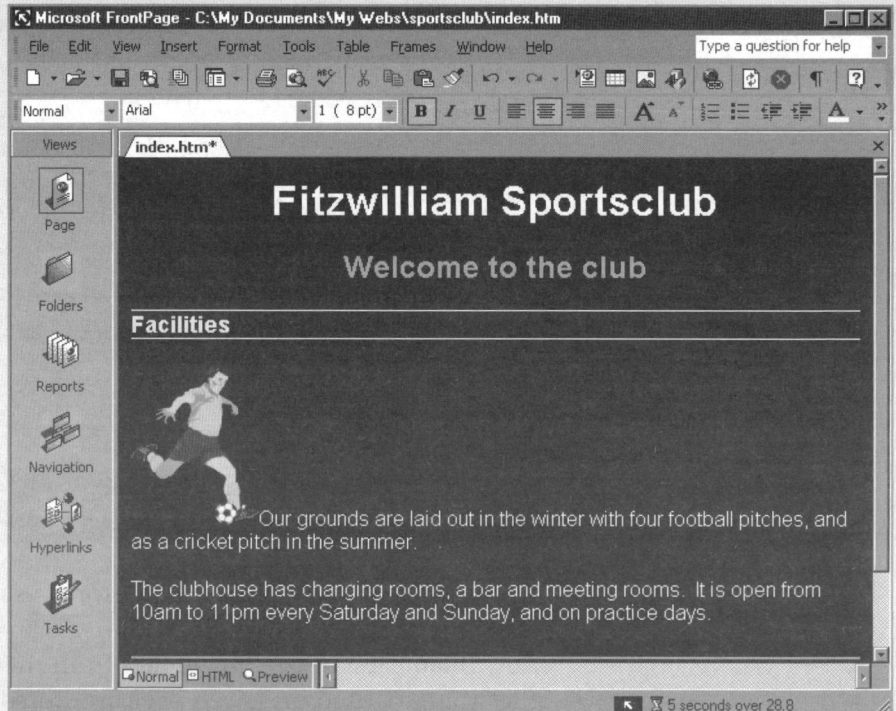

Figure 8.1 An image inserted onto a web page

3 FrontPage has already created an image folder for you. When you next save the web page, FrontPage prompts you to save the image as well, with the Save Embedded Files dialogue box shown in Figure 8.2. The image should be saved in the images folder, so if 'images/' does not appear in the Folder field, click on **Change Folder** and open the images folder.

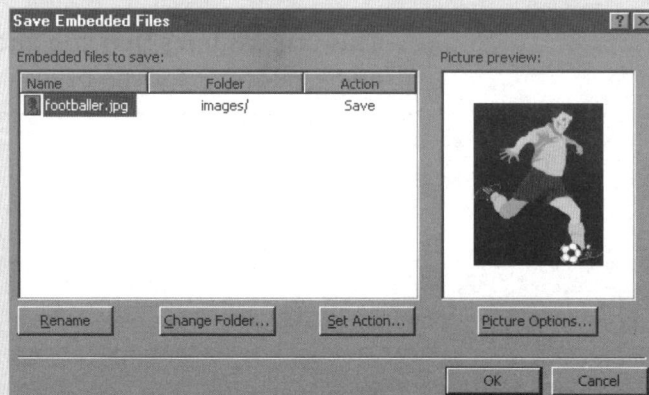

Figure 8.2 Saving an image for a web page

Hint:

A word of warning – when you are working in FrontPage do not use Windows Explorer to copy images directly into the images folder. You have to find them elsewhere, insert them on your page, then allow FrontPage to place them in the images folder.

Changing the image properties

Once an image has been placed on a page, the HTML coding includes an <img> tag, such as:

```
<img border="0" src="images/footballer.jpg" width="100"
height="127">
```

Border, source (src), width and height are all **attributes** of the <img> tag. Attributes are HTML's way of listing the properties of the image.

> ## Information
>
> - **src** is the filename of the image and its location relative to the page.
> - **width** and **height** are the dimensions of the image. Altering these values will distort the image but will not change the memory needed.

Images cannot be manipulated as simply as they can in DTP packages, but further attributes can be added to the <img> tag. Most web authoring packages provide an image properties dialogue box, usually accessed by right-clicking the image in page edit mode, and this generates more attributes, such as:

```
<img border="0" src="images/footballer.jpg" alt="A footballer"
align="right" hspace="10" width="100" height="127">
```

See the effect of these in Figure 8.3.

> ## Information
>
> - **alt** text appears as a screen label in a browser, when the mouse is held over an image, see Figure 8.3. This acts as a marker if an image is slow to download and it also provides a useful description to the visitor. Alt text is essential to make a site accessible to blind visitors, who will use text readers to understand the content.
> - **align** positions the image relative to the text next to it – the effect depends entirely on where the cursor was placed when the image was inserted.
> - **border** values greater than zero draw a border around the image, with the given thickness measured in pixels.
> - **hspace** (horizontal)and **vspace** (vertical) create space around the image.

Method

1   In Normal mode, right-click on the image and select **Picture Properties**. Any changes that you make to the properties of an image will be listed as <img> attributes in the HTML code.

2   In the Picture Properties dialogue box, select the General tab, and enter some descriptive text in the **Alternative Representations Text** box. This is the 'alt' text for the image.

3   Next, click on the **Appearance** tab. Do not alter the size properties, but experiment with the Layout properties. All the values are in pixels.

4   When you have made your selections view the page in Preview mode (Figure 8.3).

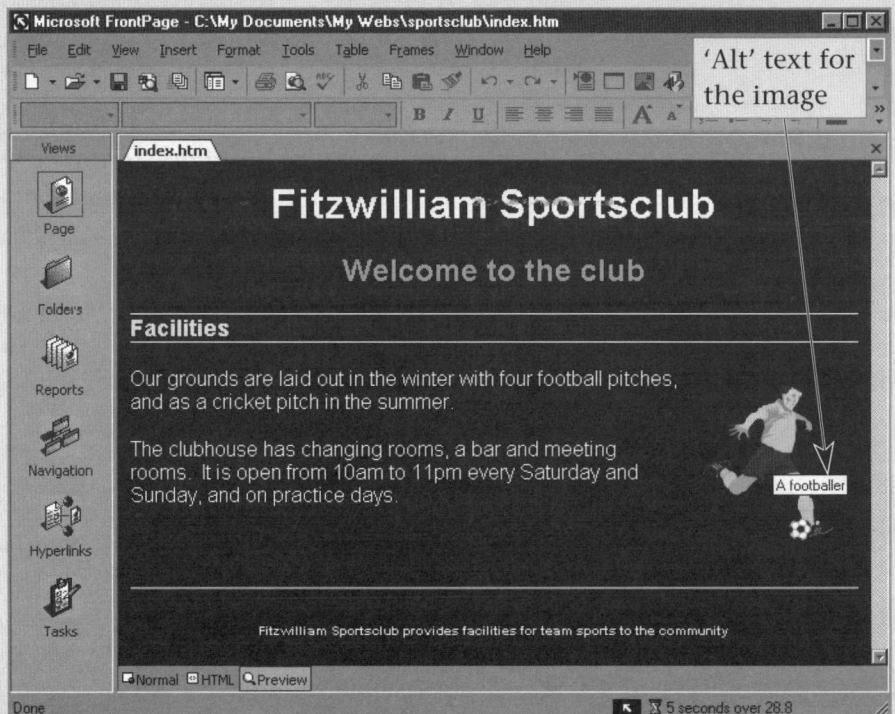

Figure 8.3 The effect of changing the properties of an image

Manipulating images on a web page

Normally you should manipulate images (change size, colours etc.) in a graphics package. FrontPage does have some simple image manipulation features built-in, but they must be used with some care.

Information

You can insert clip art on a web page just as you can in word processing or desktop publishing documents. You can then use the inbuilt image manipulation tools to change it.

Method

1 Click on the page where you want the clip art to appear. Select **Insert**, **Picture**, then **Clip Art**, and choose the clip art image that you want. It will be inserted on the page.

2 The clip art image will probably have to be changed before it is right for your page (see Figure 8.4).

3 Click on the image, and the Pictures toolbar will appear at the bottom of the window.

4 You can use the buttons on the Pictures toolbar to rotate or flip the image. You can also change the brightness and contrast of the colours.

5 If you want to go back to the original drawing, click on the Restore button.

Hint:

The clip art image will look odd if the background colour of the page is different from the background colour of the gif. A technique will be explained later for overcoming this by making the background of the gif transparent.

Hint:

You can make images smaller using the image manipulation features of FrontPage. Although you can also make images larger they will not look good, as they will lose their definition.

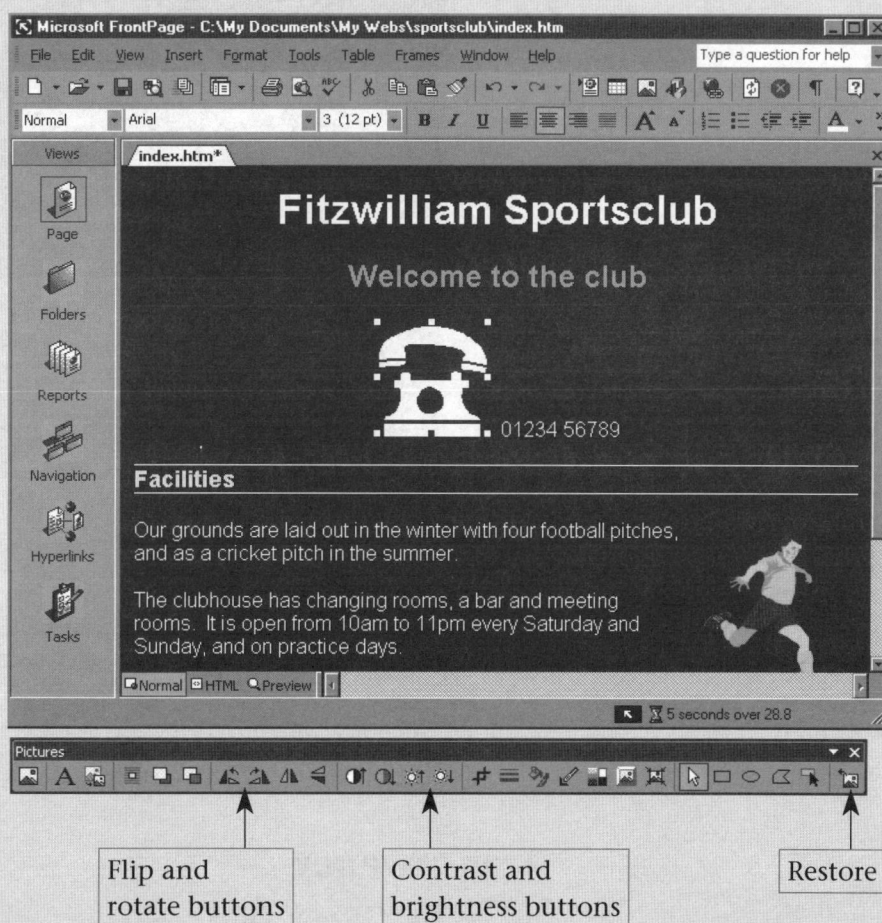

Figure 8.4 Clip art inserted on the page, showing the Pictures toolbar at bottom

Information

FrontPage allows you to manipulate images to a certain extent without using specialist graphics packages. You can resize an image directly on the page, but you must resample it to save it again at its new dimensions. This ensures that the image file is no larger than it need to be.

FrontPage will also convert an image to a gif or jpg for you automatically when you save it.

Making an image smaller in FrontPage

Method

1 Resize the clip art image you used before by dragging on the corner handles. If you drag on one of the side handles the image will be squashed in one direction only. If you drag on one of the corner handles the image will get smaller but still keep the same proportions. The image may look a little distorted at this stage.

2 Click on the image, then click on the **Resample** button 🔳 from the **Pictures** toolbar. Not only does this reduce the size of the image file but it also improves the appearance of the image (Figure 8.5).

Figure 8.5 The corner handles have been used to resize the image

<table>
<tr><td></td></tr>
</table>

3 Save the page. The Save Embedded Files dialogue box will appear. The name of the images folder should appear under **Folder**. If the word images does not appear under Folder, then click on **Change Folder**, and select the images folder.

4 FrontPage will convert the image to gif format and then save the image as a separate file in the images folder.

Hint:

You can check which image files have been saved by clicking on the images folder in the Folders list.

Transparency

In Figure 8.5 the telephone image has a black background so it fits on the black background of the page. But most clip art, and many other images, has a white background, so the image can look very odd on the page (Figure 8.6).

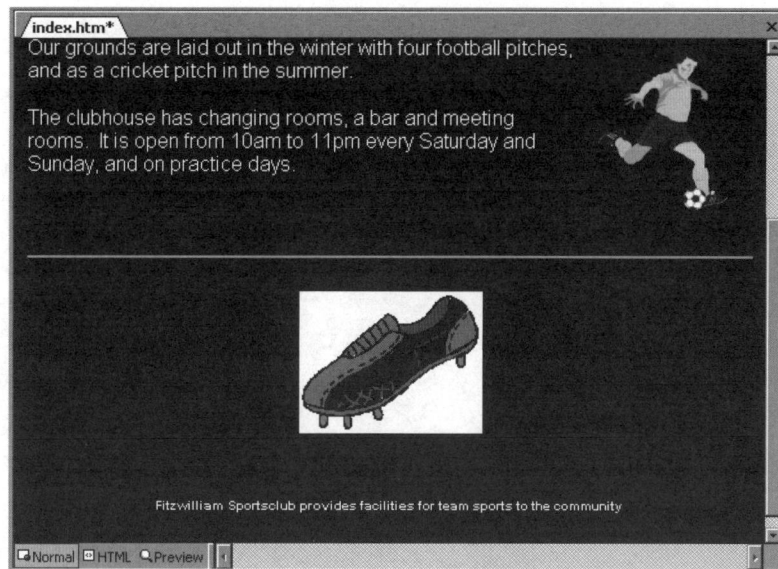

Figure 8.6 This image has the wrong colour background

In gif format you can make the background of the image transparent so that the background colour of the page shows through. You can do this in any graphics package that generates gifs. Some web authoring packages allow you to do this to the image directly on the page.

Task 8.5   Using transparency

You can experiment with transparency by inserting clip art.

Method

1   Click on the page where you want the clip art to be placed. Select **Insert**, **Picture**, then **Clip Art**, and choose a clip art image that has a different colour background from the background on your page.

2   Click on the image then click on the **Set Transparent Color** button. You may get a message at this point – if so, click on OK.

3   Now click on the background of the image. In the example in Figure 8.6, you would click somewhere in the white area. The background of the image will become transparent, and show the background colour of the page (Figure 8.7).

4   Save the page and the image as before.

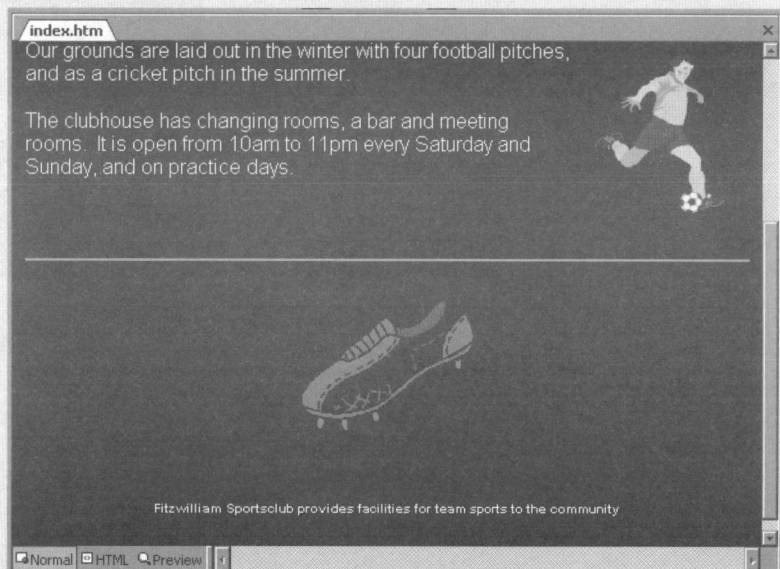

Figure 8.7 The image now has a transparent background

Converting a bitmap image

All images have to be saved in a compressed format to be usable on a web page. In FrontPage it is possible to insert an image that is in an uncompressed bitmap (bmp) format. You can then use FrontPage to convert the image to a gif or jpg. This is particularly useful if you want to use a photo that is in bitmap format.

Task 8.6	Converting a bitmap file into a jpg file

Method

1. Click on the page at the point where you want to insert the image. Select **Insert**, **Picture**, then **From File**. Click on the folder icon and browse to the location of your bitmap image.
2. Resize the image as before. Resample it.
3. Save the page. In the **Save Embedded Files** dialogue box, click on **Picture Options**.
4. In the Picture Options dialogue box you can choose whether to save the image as a JPEG or GIF. Select JPEG and select 75 for **Quality**.

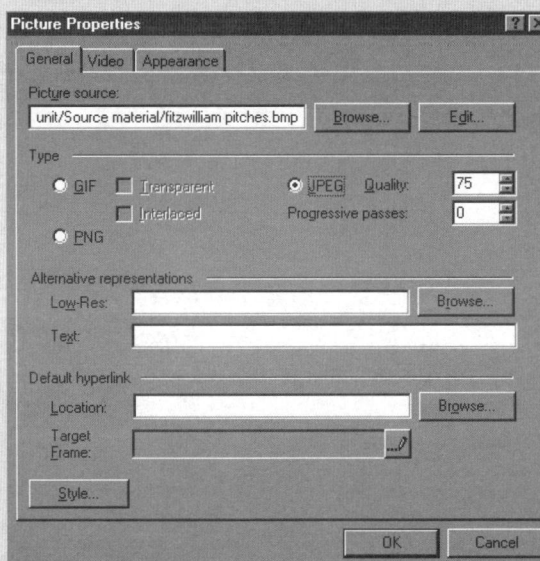

Figure 8.8 Converting a bitmap to a jpg

Background images

A background image can be applied to a page instead of a background colour, although backgrounds should be chosen carefully because too much detail can distract a visitor from the text. All backgrounds are automatically **tiled**, that is, repeated to fill the space, so quite a small image can be used.

Web authoring packages usually provide a selection of background images, which are defined in the HTML like this:

```
<body background="images/ripple.gif">
```

Background images are usually only successful if they are very subtle.

Task 8.7 | Adding a background image

Method

1 To change the background image on a page, select **Background** in the **Format** menu.
2 In the Background tab of the Page Properties dialogue box, select **Background Picture**, then browse to find a suitable image. You will probably have some background images in your clip art gallery.
3 The background image you have chosen now tiles across the whole page (Figure 8.9).

Figure 8.9 Unsuitable use of background images

Thumbnails

A thumbnail is a small image that links to a larger version of the image. Thumbnails are often used to display high quality photos on a website. The full size photo may take some time to download, so a smaller image (thumbnail) is displayed on the page and the visitor can then choose whether or not to download it. Usually the thumbnail acts as a graphical button, and the visitor clicks on it to view the full size image.

FrontPage simplifies the process of creating thumbnails.

Task 8.8 — Creating a thumbnail

Method

1 Click on the page at the point where you want to insert the thumbnail. Select **Insert**, **Picture**, then **From File**. Click on the folder icon and browse to the location of your photo.

2 The full size photo will eventually be replaced by a thumbnail, and the original photo will be displayed on a separate page. For the moment the full size photo appears in the position where the thumbnail will appear, so it may look a little odd. You may need to resize the full size photo, but this is not necessary if it is already of a size that will fit into a single web page. Resample the photo if you resize it.

3 Save the page and the photo before you go on to the next step, as in Task 8.6.

4 Click on the photo, then click on the **Auto Thumbnail** button 🖼 in the Pictures toolbar. The full size photo will be replaced by a thumbnail version.

5 Save the page. You will be prompted to save the thumbnail image.

6 You can change the appearance of the thumbnail by right-clicking on the image and selecting **Picture Properties**. Don't forget to add some 'alt' text.

7 In Preview mode, click on the thumbnail, and the full size image should appear.

8 It is a good idea to check this in a browser as well, so save the page and select **Preview in Browser** from the File menu.

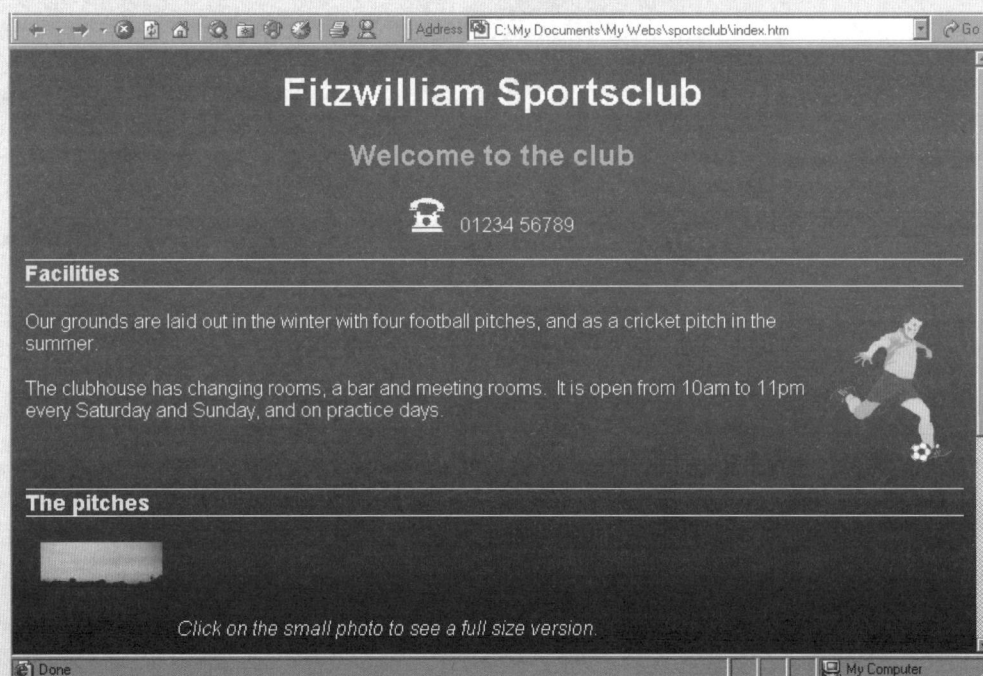

Figure 8.10 A page with a thumbnail viewed in a browser

Figure 8.11 The full size photo appears in the browser when the thumbnail is clicked

→ Practise your skills 1

1 Open the web that you were working on in the Practise your skills exercises for Section 7.

2 Insert a suitable piece of clip art on the home page.

3 Use the functions on the Picture toolbar to manipulate the image, for example, to reduce it in size, rotate it, and alter the contrast and brightness.

4 Resample the image.

5 Save the page and, when prompted, save the image in the images folder.

6 Use the Picture Properties to, for example, add or remove a border, add space around the image.

7 Use the Picture Properties to add 'alt' text to the image.

8 Save the page again.

→ Practise your skills 2

1 In the same web as used in the Practise your skills exercises for Section 7, insert another clip art image, but choose one in which the background is a different colour from the background of the page.

2 Make the background of the image transparent.

3 Save the page and the image.

→ Practise your skills 3

1 For this exercise you need to have a set of digital photos. These could be on a photo CD, or could be ones that you have uploaded from a digital camera.

2 In the same web as used in the last Practise your skills section, use your template to create a new page for the site. This will hold the photo gallery.

3 Insert a photo on the page. This needs to be replaced by a thumbnail. But first you should, if necessary, resize and resample the original photo.

4 If the photo is a bitmap, then use the Picture Properties to change it to a jpg.

5 Create a thumbnail of the photo.

6 Save the page and image.

7 Check that the thumbnail works in a browser.

8 Add a second thumbnail to the page. Continue to do this with other photos.

9 Create a link from the index page to this page. You can create your own button, by clicking on the **Insert** menu, then selecting **Component**, then **Hover Button**.

10 Save the web – you will use it again in the Practise your skills exercises for Section 9.

→ Check your knowledge

1 What is the 'alt' attribute of an image?

2 What is a thumbnail?

Section 9

Using tables and bookmarks to aid layout

You will learn to

- Use tables to enhance the layout of text and graphics
- Use anchors (bookmarks) to establish hyperlinks within a single web page

Using tables for layout

Tables can be used to hold tabular data, as we saw in Section 2. On web pages, tables are often used for another purpose – to create a layout for a page. In this way, the text and images can be placed on a page relative to each other. It is also possible to use a table to fix positions exactly so that nothing moves when the window is resized.

Task 9.1 Starting a new website with FrontPage

For this activity you will create a website for a local group. You will use a cascading style sheet to give the page its style and will later add a separate side frame to hold the navigation bar.

Hint:

It is a good idea to work in a screen resolution of 1024 wide. The pages will be designed to be viewed at 800 resolution, but by using a wider window in FrontPage you will also be able to see the Views bar and the Task Pane at the same time as the page itself.

Method

1. Create a new empty web, giving it a suitable name.
2. Select **File**, **New**, **Page or Web**, then select **Page Templates**. Click on the **Style Sheets** tab. Select the 'Street' style sheet template and save it as mystyles.css.
3. Create and save a template based on your style sheet.
4. Create a new page based on the template and save it as homepage.htm. Although this will be the home page for the site it will not actually be the first page that is loaded, so is not saved as index.htm.

Understanding the width of tables and cells

You may want to control the behaviour of tables by fixing the size of various components.

The <table> tag can be given a number of size attributes, such as:

```
<table width="600" border="1" cellspacing="3" cellpadding="5">
```

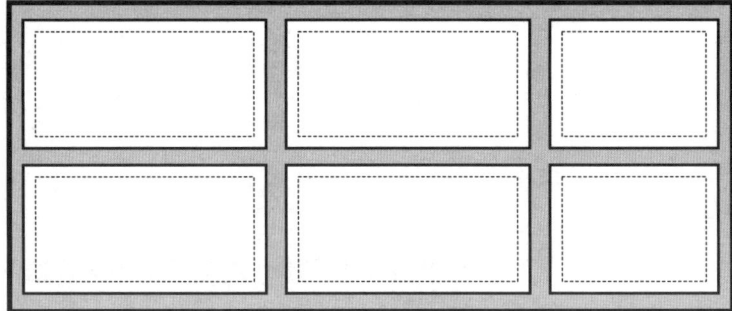

Figure 9.1 Table components

> **Hint:**
>
> In FrontPage you can set table attributes by right-clicking inside a table in Normal Mode, then selecting Table Properties.

> **Information**
>
> - **width** is the total width of the table.
> - **border** is the width in pixels of the border around the outside of the table.
> - **cell spacing** is the width in pixels between the border and a cell, or between one cell and another, and is shown shaded in Figure 9.1.
> - **cell padding** is the width of the space inside a cell between the edge of the cell and the text. The limit of this is shown by a dotted line in Figure 9.1, although it is usually invisible.

The width can also be set for an individual cell in a table:

```
<td width="200">
```

or

```
<td width="40%">
```

> **Hint:**
>
> In FrontPage you can set attributes of an individual cell by right-clicking inside a cell in Normal Mode, then selecting Cell Properties.

> **Information**
>
> - **width** is the width of the cell inside the cell padding. It can be given in pixels or as a percentage of the total width of the table.

It is only necessary to set the cell widths for one row (any row) in the table, as all the cells in any one column will line up under each other.

Method

1. Open the home page that you created in Task 9.1.
2. Select **Table**, **Insert**, then **Table** and enter values in the dialogue box as in Figure 9.2. Note that the width is given in pixels, not percentage. This gives a table with two rows and three columns.

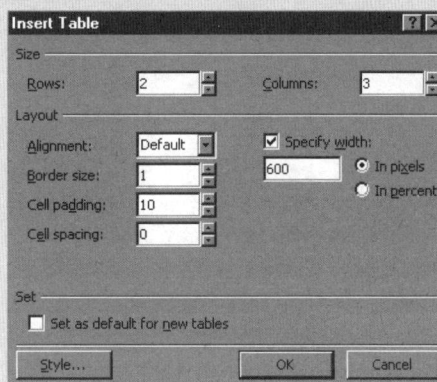

Figure 9.2 Inserting a table in FrontPage

3. In Normal mode enter text in some of the cells and place images in other cells. If necessary, reduce the images to a suitable size and resample them.
4. To add an extra row to a table, click in the row immediately above or below where you want it to go. Select **Table**, **Insert**, then **Rows** and make your choices. You can add a new column in the same way.
5. Save the page and images. See Figure 9.3 for an example of a table with an extra row added.

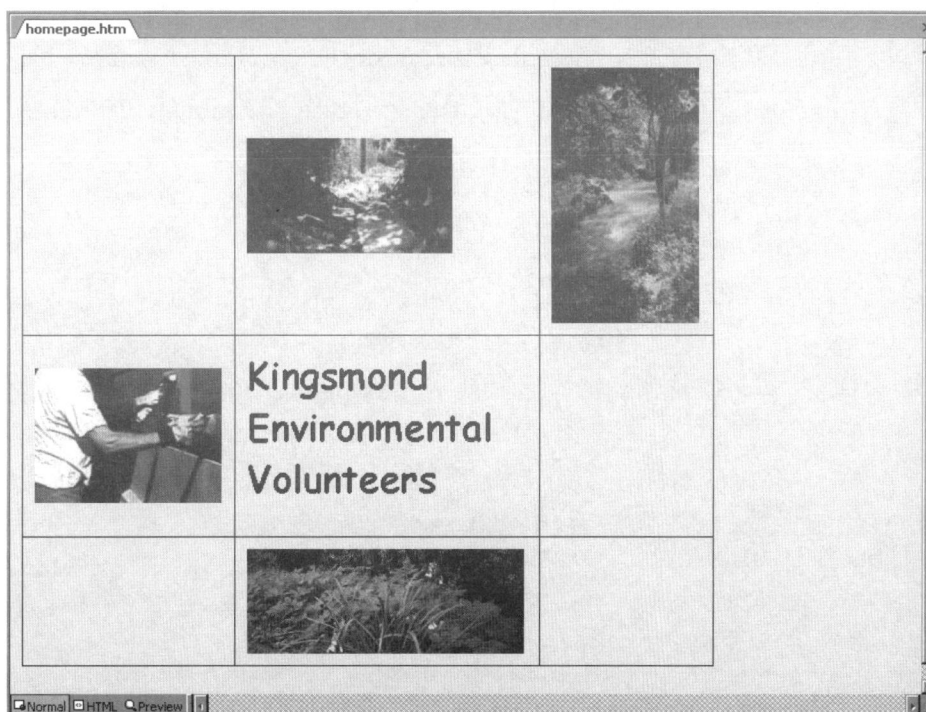

Figure 9.3 A table used to layout text and graphics

The HTML for the table shown in Figure 9.3 is like this:

```
<table border="1" cellpadding="10" cellspacing="0"
width="600">
<tr>
<td> </td>
<td>
<img border="0" src="images/litter.jpg" width="178"
height="100">
</td>
<td><img border="0" src="images/stream.jpg" width="130"
height="222">
</td>
</tr>
<tr>
<td><img border="0" src="images/graffiti.jpg" width="160"
height="117">
</td>
<td>
<h1>Kingsmond<br>
Environmental<br>
Volunteers</h1>
</td>
<td> </td>
</tr>
<tr>
<td> </td>
<td><img border="0" src="images/plants.jpg" width="240"
height="91">
</td>
<td> </td>
</tr>
</table>
```

Merging cells

A group of cells can also be merged together for layout purposes. For example, you can merge the cells in the top row of a table to create a heading across all the columns of a table.

In HTML the structure of a table with merged cells is like this:

```
<table>
<tr>
<td colspan="3"> </td>
</tr>
<tr>
<td> </td>
<td> </td>
<td> </td>
</tr>
<tr>
<td> </td>
<td> </td>
<td> </td>
</tr>
</table>
```

Note that the three cells in the first row have been replaced by one cell which spans all three columns.

You can also merge cells in a column down several rows.

Task 9.3 | Merging cells

Method

1　Open the page used in Task 9.2.
2　In Normal mode, highlight the cells that you want to merge. Select **Table,** then **Merge Cells**.
3　Figure 9.4 shows how you can merge several sets of cells to give an interesting layout.

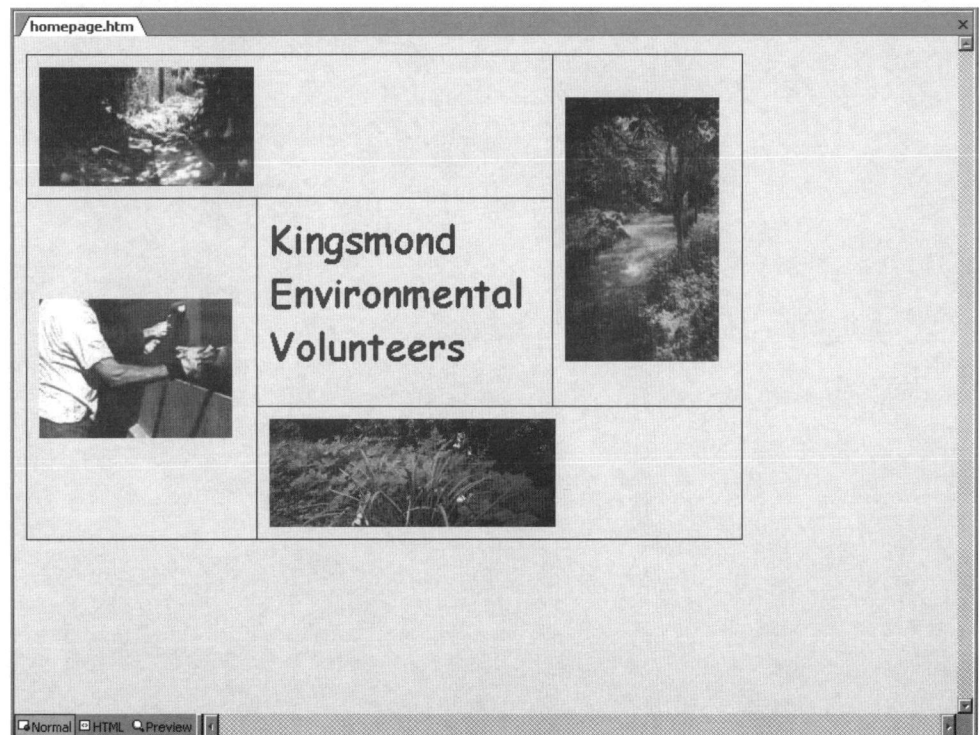

Hint:

If you merge the cells where you have set all the width properties, that width data will no longer be valid.

Figure 9.4 Cells merged

Setting other table properties

You can set other properties for tables or for individual cells, for example, background colours, text alignment and border styles. In FrontPage, right-click anywhere inside the table, then select the Table Properties or Cell Properties. If you set the border width to zero, then the table becomes invisible. This is commonly used as a way of laying out a page.

Task 9.4 | Setting table and cell properties

Method

I   Experiment with the table properties in Normal mode by right-clicking anywhere inside the table, then selecting **Table Properties**. You can add colour to the borders and change their appearance, and you can give the whole table a background colour.

Information

All tables are aligned to the left of the page by default unless you specify otherwise. For our task do not change the default value.

2   Set the table border value to zero. You will still be able to see a dotted outline of the cells in Normal mode, but this will not be visible in Preview mode.
3   Click inside a cell, and select **Cell Properties**. Use it to set the background colour for a single cell.
4   Use the Cell Properties to align the contents of the cell – text or image – vertically (top, middle or bottom) and horizontally (left, centre, right).

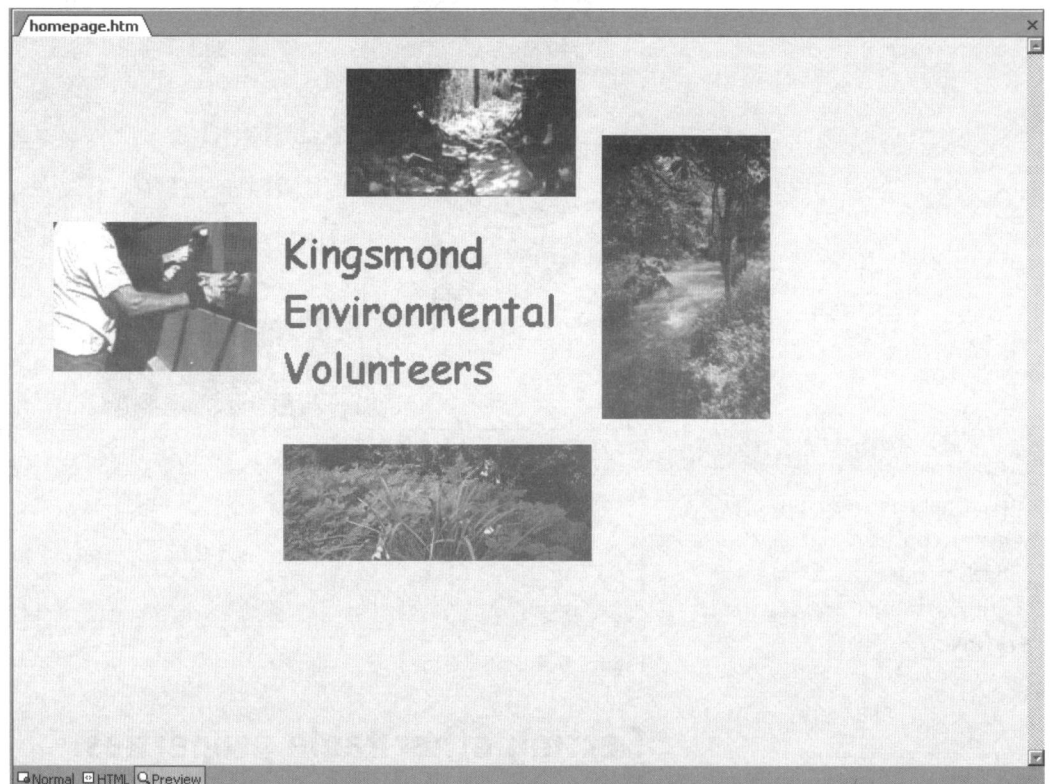

Figure 9.5 The final layout in Preview mode

The HTML code for the layout in Figure 9.5 is:

```
<table border="0" cellpadding="10" cellspacing="0"
width="600">
<tr>
<td colspan="2" valign="bottom" align="right">
<img border="0" src="images/litter.jpg" width="178"
height="100">
</td>
<td rowspan="2" valign="bottom" align="left"><img border="0"
src="images/stream.jpg" width="130" height="222">
</td>
</tr>
<tr>
<td rowspan="2" valign="top" align="right"><img border="0"
src="images/graffiti.jpg" width="160" height="117">
</td>
<td>
<h1>Kingsmond<br>
Environmental<br>
Volunteers</h1>
</td>
</tr>
<tr>
<td colspan="2" valign="top" align="left"><img border="0"
src="images/plants.jpg" width="240" height="91">
</td>
</tr>
</table>
```

Information

- **align** is the horizontal alignment (the default value is "left").
- **valign** is the vertical alignment (the default value is "middle").

Fixing the size of a page

The page you have created is completely contained within the table.

We want the page to be exactly 600 pixels wide, in order to accommodate a side frame which we will add later.

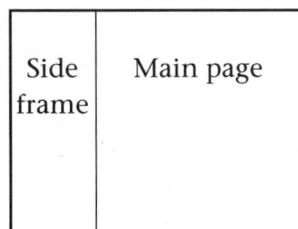

Figure 9.6 Page plan showing side frame

If you look closely at Figure 9.4 you will see that there is a small margin to the left and top of the table, making the page wider than required. These margins should be reduced to zero.

Task 9.5 Changing the page margins

Method

1 Open the page used in Task 9.4.
2 Right-click anywhere inside the page and select **Page Properties**. Click on the **Margins** tab, and set the top and left margins to 0 (Figure 9.7).

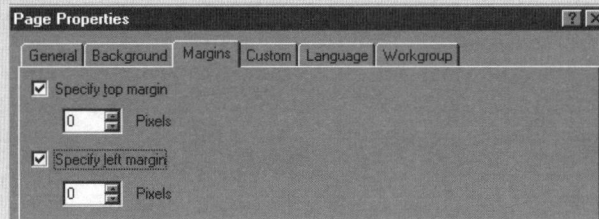

Figure 9.7 Setting the page margins to zero

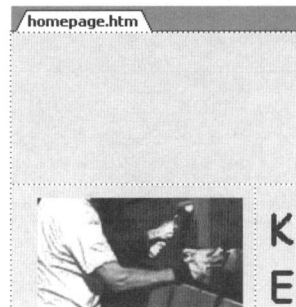

Figure 9.8 Page with margins set at zero, as viewed in Normal mode

Using a table with only one cell

You can create a table with only one row and one column to contain the contents of a page. If this table is then given a width in pixels then the width of the page is fixed.

If the browser window is made narrower than the fixed width of the page, then the visitor will have to scroll horizontally to view all the page. For this reason many web designers work to a maximum window size of 800 pixels.

Information

The best page width to use is 800 pixels. In practice, however, the width of the scrollbar to the right of the page uses up some of the screen width, so it is better to set the width at 780 pixels. A table of width 780 can be used as a container for a full page. In our example the main page is 600 pixels wide and the side frame will be 180 pixels wide, making a total width of 780 pixels.

If the browser window is wider than the fixed width of the page then blank space is displayed. If the table that holds the page is aligned to the left (the default) then the extra space appears to the right. If the table is aligned to the centre, then space appears on both sides. Pages are not normally aligned to the right because the eyes always begin looking at the left of the screen.

New tables can be placed within the single cell table, but make sure that they are not too wide to fit on the page.

| Task 9.6 | Creating a page contained within a single cell table |

Method

1. In the same web as before, add a new page based on the template, and save it.
2. Set up a table, 600 pixels wide, to hold the contents of the page. The table should have 1 row and 1 column.
3. Use the Page Properties dialogue box to set the top and left margins to zero.
4. Now add some text and images to the page.

Bookmarks

As we saw in Section 6, hyperlinks can be used to link to another page on the same website or to another website. Hyperlinks can also be used to link to positions (bookmarks) on the same page.

This is a useful technique if a page contains a lot of information and, as such, is quite long. By placing links at the top of the page to content further down, the visitor's attention is drawn to the hidden material.

Creating hyperlinks to bookmarks

In a browser a hyperlink can jump to an invisible bookmark placed elsewhere on a page. In the HTML code a bookmark is denoted with the <a> tag which has a name attribute to identify it. In this HTML example, a heading with the title 'First section' has been bookmarked so that a hyperlink somewhere else on the page can link to it:

```
<h2><a name="First section">First section</a></h2>
```

The text that is to become the hyperlink is then highlighted and formatted as a link. The HTML code for the hyperlink itself uses the <a> tag again and looks like this:

```
<p><a href="#First section">Link to first section</a></p>
```

| Task 9.7 | Creating links to bookmarks |

Method

1. On the new page that you created, enter information in at least two sections, each with a subheading. The links to these sections will be placed at the top of the page.

2   To insert a bookmark, highlight the first subheading to be bookmarked, and select **Insert** then **Bookmark**. By default, this gives the bookmark the same name as the subheading. A bookmark is displayed in Normal mode by a dotted underlining (as in Figure 9.9), but is invisible in Preview mode.

3   Now highlight the text that will act as the hyperlink, and select **Insert** then **Hyperlink**. In the dialogue box, click on **Bookmark**, then select the relevant bookmark from the Bookmark list, as in Figure 9.10.

4   Add the remaining hyperlinks (Figure 9.11) then try them out in Preview mode.

5   You can use a graphic as a hyperlink to a bookmark. Insert a suitable image, then highlight it and select **Insert** then **Hyperlink** in exactly the same way as you did with text.

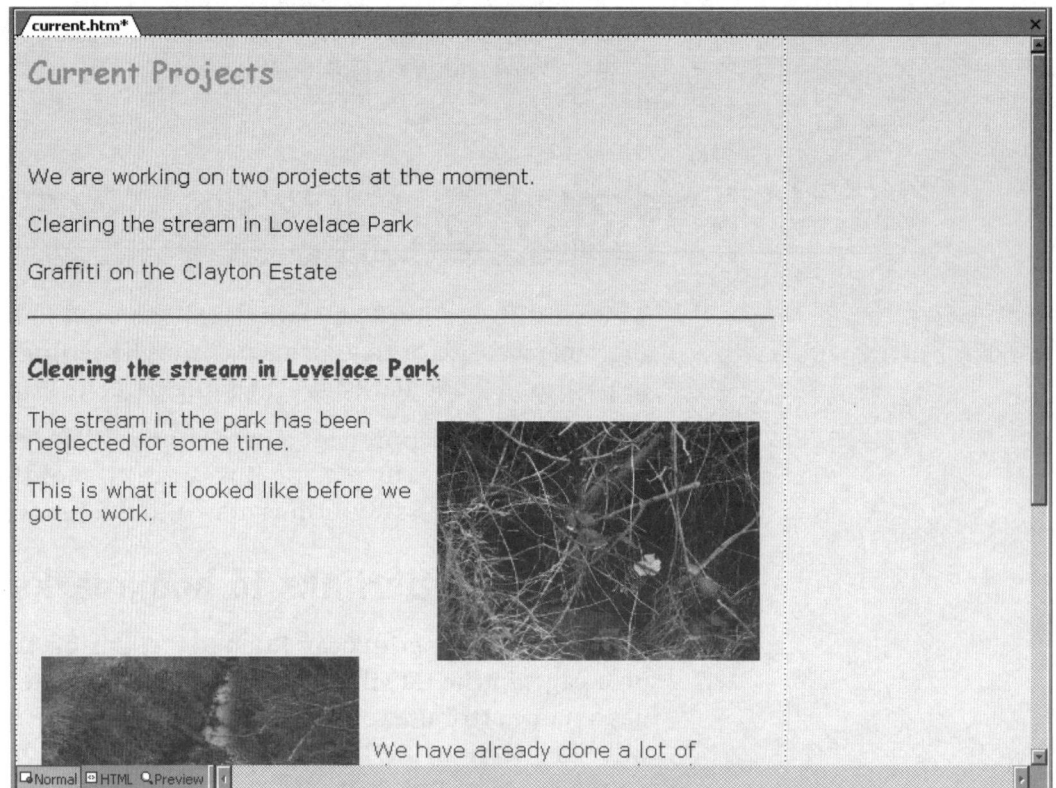

Figure 9.9 The subheading has been bookmarked in Normal mode

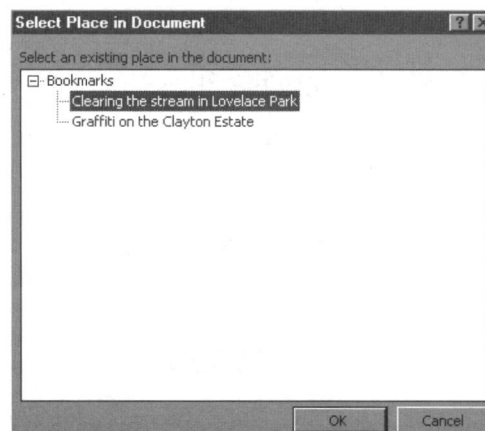

Figure 9.10 Selecting a bookmark that the hyperlink will link to

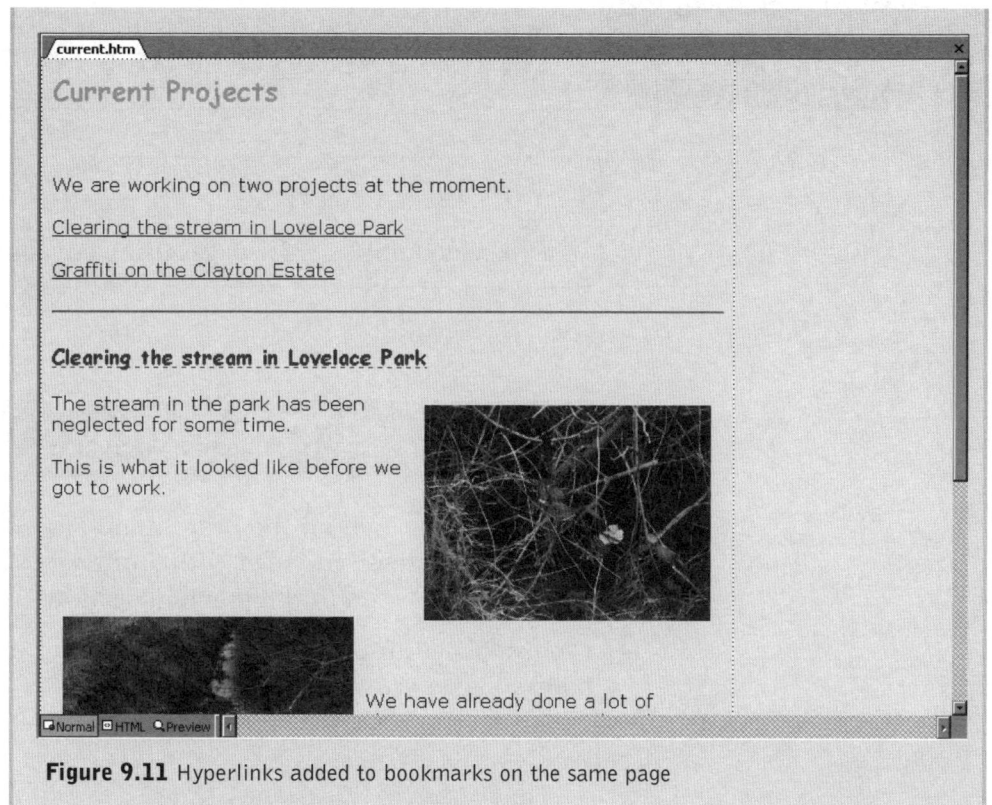

Figure 9.11 Hyperlinks added to bookmarks on the same page

→ Practise your skills 1

1 Open the web that you were using for the Practise your skills exercises in Section 8.
2 Using your storyboard as a guide, create the third page.
3 Set up a table and use it to layout text and images on the page.
4 Set the border of the table to zero.
5 Check the page in a browser.
6 Add links to this page from the other pages, and add suitable links from this page.

→ Practise your skills 2

1 From your storyboard, use the template to create the final page in your web.
2 Enter the information on the page, with subheadings.
3 Use the subheadings to create bookmarks. Add links to the bookmarks at the top of the page.

→ Check your knowledge

1 Explain cell spacing and cell padding as they relate to tables.
2 What are the advantages of using a table to lay out the contents of a web page?
3 What is a bookmark?

More about style sheets

You will learn to

- Create templates for pages using advanced style sheets

Looking at style sheets

The style sheet used on the Kingsmond Environmental Volunteers web is one of the samples provided with FrontPage, called 'Street'. The effect of this style sheet was seen in the previous section.

Each style definition refers to one or more of the HTML tags. This is the body style definition in the style sheet:

```
body
{
    font-family: Verdana, Arial, Helvetica;
    background-color: rgb(204,255,255);
    color: rgb(0,0,102);
}
```

This defines some properties that apply to the whole page between the <body> tags. The Normal style that can be selected from the style list is the default style, and this is initially defined by the system settings for the computer. The body style definition sets up the basic style for the page, and a browser will use this as the default style.

Information

- **background-color** (note the American spelling of colour) applies to the background of the whole page.
- **color** defines the default colour for the text on the page. This is expressed as a RGB (Red, Green, Blue) colour code. Each of the three colour numbers can take a value from 0 (none of that colour) to 255 (full colour).
- **font-family**, in this case, lists three fonts, although the list can be of any length. The browser works along the list until it finds a font that it can use.

The visitor can only view a font if that font is already installed on their own system. So although in this case the designer would prefer the visitor to view the text in Verdana, the other two fonts are listed as fall back options. Only widely used fonts should be included in a style sheet, but as a precaution two basic fonts can be added to each definition, one font for Windows systems and one for Apple systems. If the preferred font is a serif font then Times New Roman and Times should be included; if the preferred font is sans serif then Arial and Helvetica should be added.

Another style definition applies to more than one tag.

```
h1,h2,h3,h4,h5,h6
{
    font-family: Comic Sans MS, Arial, Helvetica;
}
```

The Heading 1 style in the style list generates the <h1> tag in the HTML, and so on. This style rule applies to all six heading tags and sets Comic Sans MS as the font for all the headings, with Arial and Helvetica as the fall back options.

The browser has to deal with the seeming contradiction between the font properties for the body and for the headings. The font defined for the body is the default font and applies throughout the page *except* where another tag defines it differently. So the Verdana font is used everywhere except in the headings where Comic Sans is used.

The next style rule defines the colour of one of the headings, and there are similar rules for all the remaining heading styles.

```
h1
{
    color: rgb(153,0,0);
}
```

The <h1> tag has been used in Figure 10.1 for the central text 'Kingsmond Environmental Volunteers'.

By default, heading styles are always bold, and the sizes decrease from h1 to h6.

The next style definitions define three states that the hyperlinks take. The <a> tag is used for both bookmarks and hyperlinks, but these styles only affect the hyperlinks themselves.

```
a:link
{
    color: rgb(0,102,102);
}
a:visited
{
    color: rgb(0,153,153);
}
a:active
{
    color: rgb(255,102,0);
}
```

Information

- **a:link** is the normal style used for the hyperlink.
- **a:visited** is the style used for a hyperlink that has already been followed.
- **a:active** is the style used when the mouse button is held down on a hyperlink.
- **a:hover** (not used in this example) is the style used when the mouse passes over the hyperlink.

The link to the Kingsmond Herald at the bottom of the window in Figure 10.1 uses the <a> tag, and can take on one of three different colours.

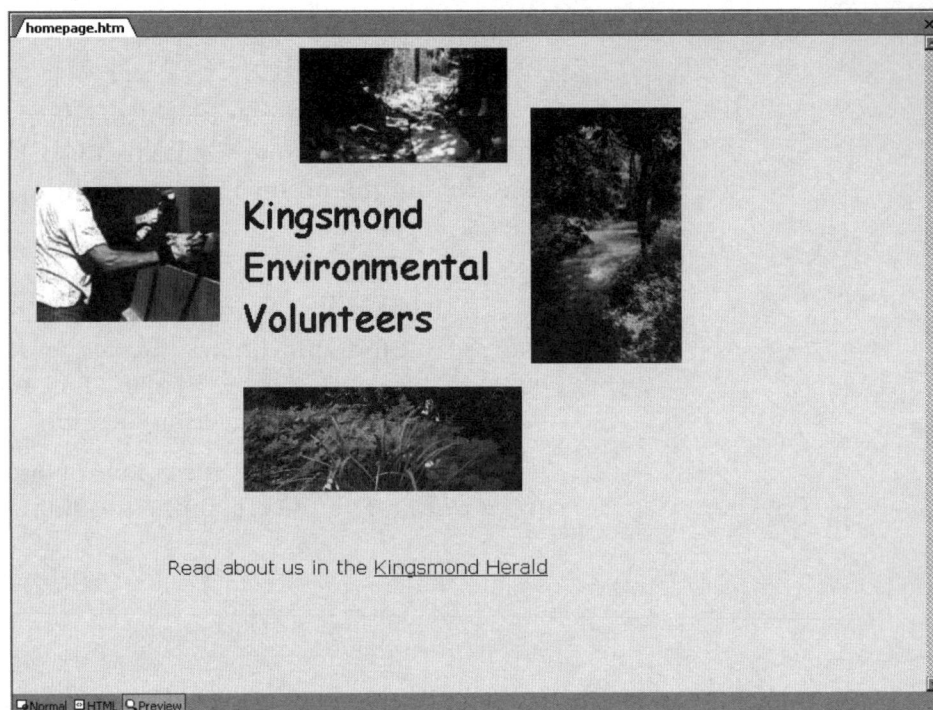

Figure 10.1 The Street style sheet applied to a page

Editing style sheets

A pre-designed style sheet can be modified. This can be done by amending the text in the style sheet file. In FrontPage the process can be simplified by using the Style dialogue box.

The HTML for a new style sheet could look like this:

```
a:link
{
    font-weight: bold;
    color: gray;
    text-decoration: none;
}
a:visited
{
    font-weight: bold;
    color: gray;
    text-decoration: none;
}
a:hover
{
    font-weight: bold;
    color: silver;
    text-decoration: none;
}
body
{
    font-family: Verdana, Arial, Helvetica;
    font-size: 12pt;
    background-color: white;
    color: rgb(0,102,51);
}
```

```
h1
{
    font-family: Comic Sans MS, Arial, Helvetica;
    font-size: 20pt;
    text-align: center;
    color: white;
    background-color: rgb(0,102,51);
    border-width: 5pt;
    border-style: double;
    border-color: white;
    padding:3pt;
}
```

Other style definitions for h2, h3 etc. can be added when needed.

Note that a style definition for a:hover has been added, and that some of the definitions have been deleted.

The effect of this style sheet can be seen in Figure 10.2. The underlining on the 'Kingsmond Herald' hyperlink has been removed, but the use of a different colour and bold face indicates to the visitor that it is a hyperlink. This is confirmed by its hover state – when the mouse is passed over the link it changes from a dark grey to a light grey.

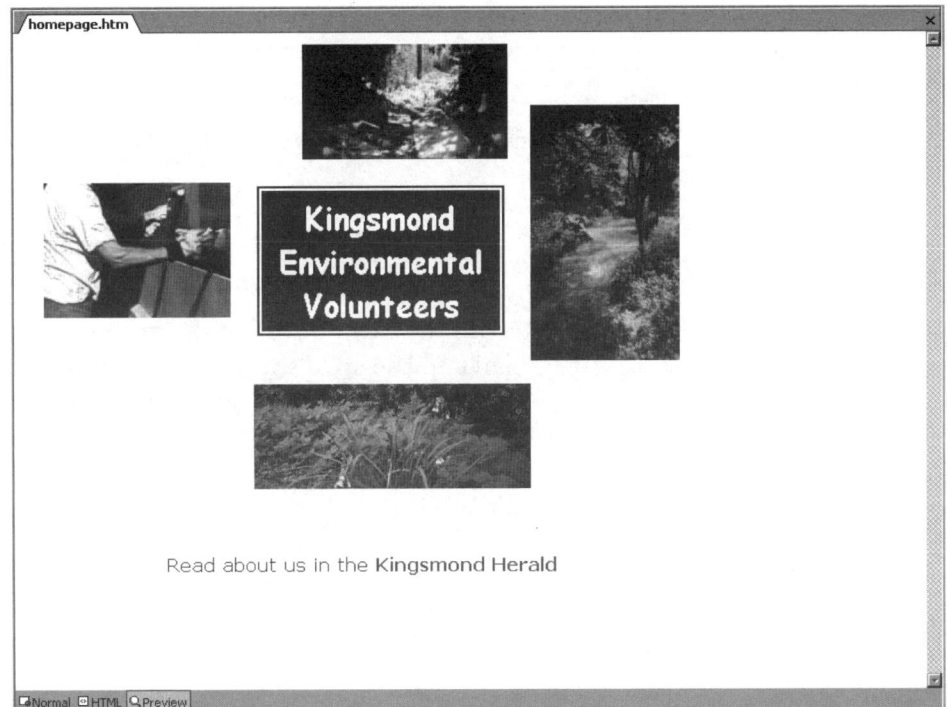

Figure 10.2 A new style sheet applied to the page

Hint:

You can change the style sheet by clicking on the Style button in the Style floating toolbar. But you can also edit the style sheet directly.

Fast and effective hover links can be created using a style sheet and without the use of images. The background, border and padding properties can be used to give a rectangular box around the text, which could change colour in hover mode.

Task 10.1 — Editing a style sheet

Method

1. First close any pages that are open, then in Folder View open mystyles.css.
2. Make changes and save it. A style sheet must be saved before any changes can be observed on a page.
3. If you amend a style sheet while a page is open, when you switch back to the page you will have to click on the Refresh button to view the effects of the changes.
4. Now use the page template to create another page for the website, in which the content should also be set inside a table 600 pixels wide. Do not include any navigation links at this stage.

Information

There are many properties that can be applied to tags in style sheet rules, and you would need to consult a handbook on Cascading Style Sheets to see them all.

→ Practise your skills 1

1. Open the four page web that you developed from a storyboard.
2. Look at the HTML code for the style sheet you set up.
3. Analyse the style definitions that you created.
4. Use the extra information from this section to make any changes you like to the style sheet. You can amend the style sheet directly in the HTML window, or you can use the Style button.

Section 11 | Creating frames

You will learn to

● Create a page layout using frames

Frames

Hint:

When using frames you should not use the Navigation tool in FrontPage.

Frames can be created directly in HTML. The process is quite complex so there is much to be said for using a web authoring package.

Frames are created in a frame page, which sets down the sizes and properties of all the frames that are being used. The frame page is always loaded first, so it is usually the index page for a website. The frame page creates the empty structure and then loads the pages into each of the frames.

Task 11.1 | Creating frames

Working with the same web as before, you will create a vertical navigation bar which will appear in a frame to the left side of the page. This frame will be 180 pixels wide, so that it will sit alongside the 600 pixels wide main frame. The total width of 780 pixels allows for the scrollbar to the right side of an 800 width window.

Method

1	First create a new page, using the page template, and save it as side.htm. Use the Page Properties dialogue box to set the page margins to zero.
2	Create a table 180 pixels wide, with one column, and one row. The cell padding should be non-zero, so that text is not pushed up against the sides of the frame.
3	Enter an image or some information at the top. See Figure 11.1 for an example of how the side page might look. Do not add any links yet.

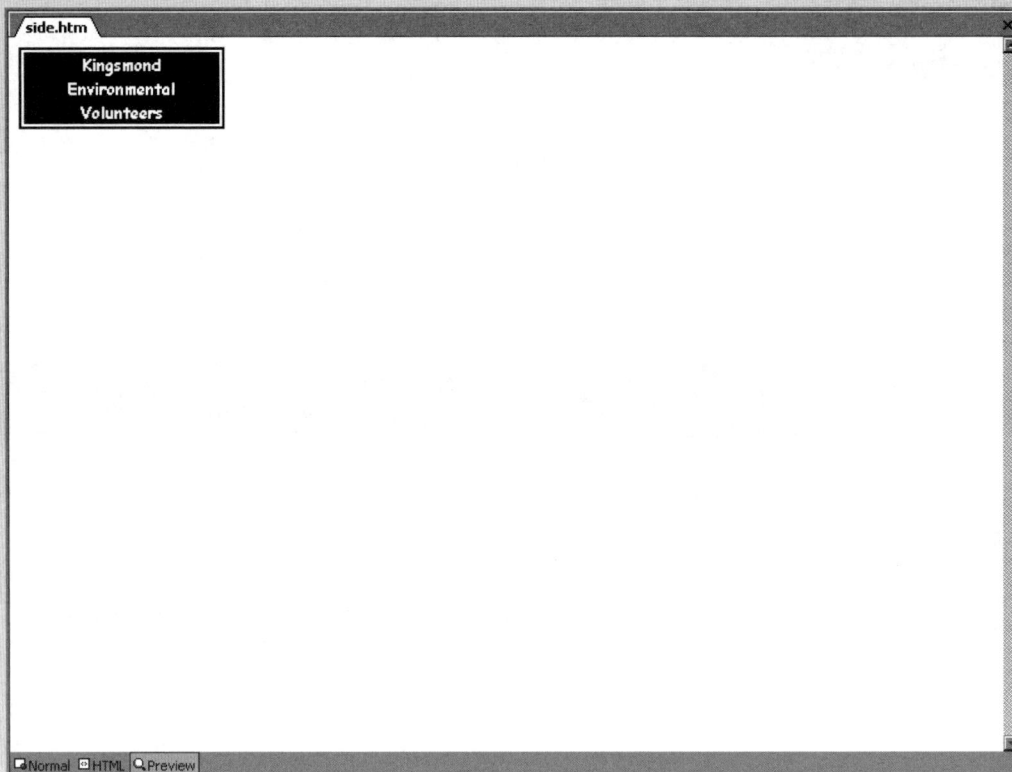

Figure 11.1 A navigation page before it has been integrated into a frame

Next the frame page itself will be created.

4   Select **File**, **New**, **Page or Web**, then select **Page Templates**. Click on the **Frames Pages** tab. Select the
      Contents template. The frame structure will appear as in Figure 11.2. Save the page as index.htm.

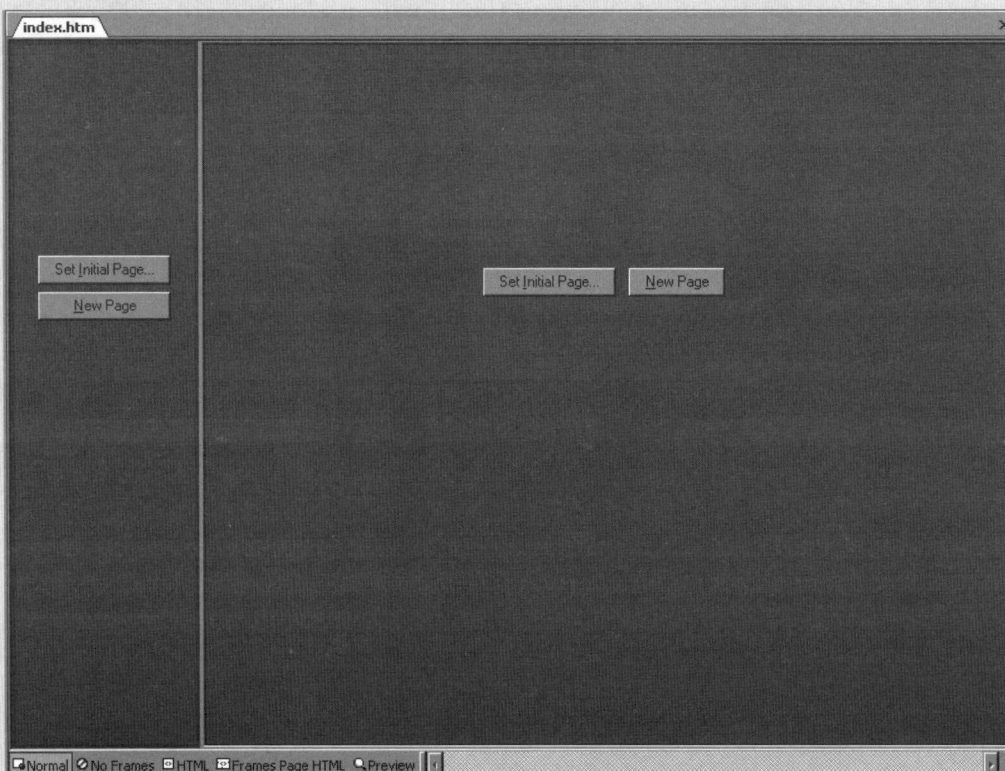

Figure 11.2 The frame structure displayed in FrontPage

5   Right-click anywhere in the left frame, and click on **Frame Properties**. Set the width to 180 pixels, and both the margins to zero. Under **Options**, you do not want the frame to be resizable so remove the tick. You also do not want a scrollbar to appear in this frame, so for **Show Scrollbars** select **Never**. The Frame Properties dialogue box should appear as in Figure 11.3.

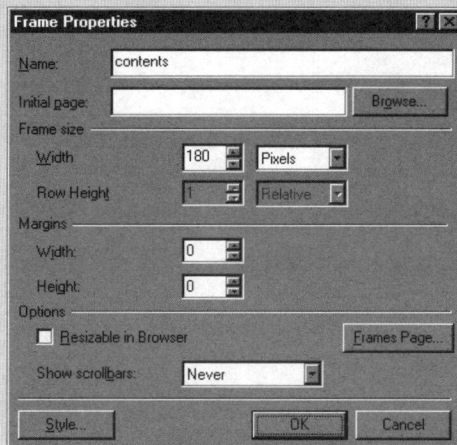

Figure 11.3 The Frame Properties dialogue box in FrontPage

6   In the right frame simply set the margins to zero.
7   In the left frame, click on **Set Initial Page**, then select side.htm. Similarly, select homepage.htm for the right frame. Save the frame page again.
8   View the whole frame page by selecting Preview mode (Figure 11.4).

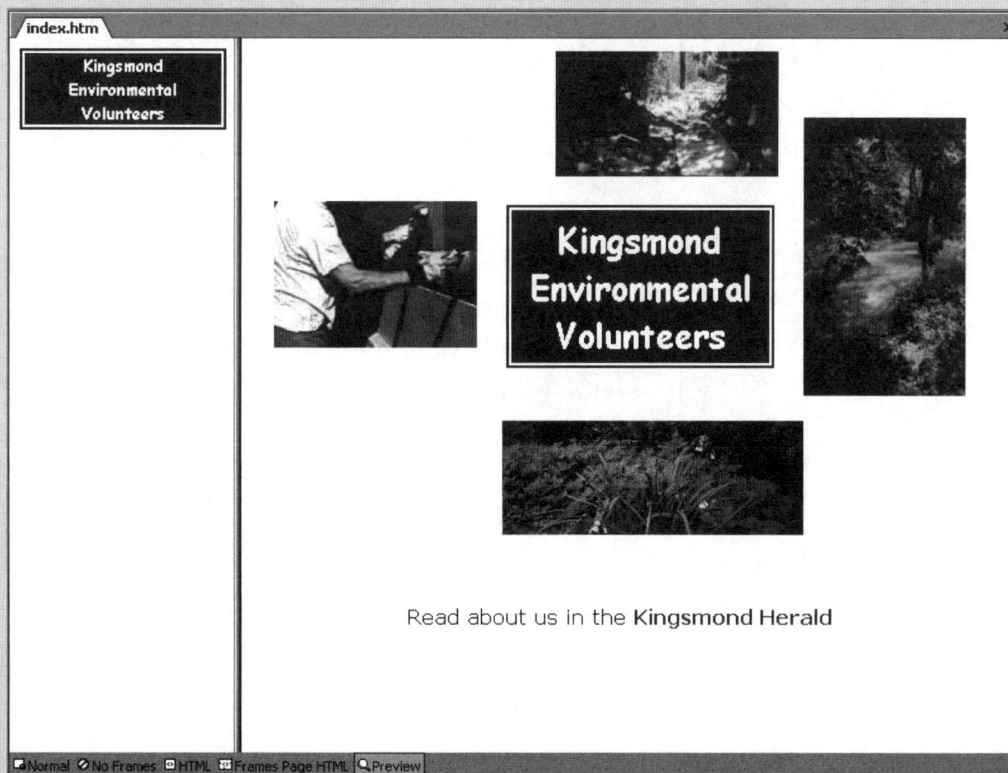

Figure 11.4 A two frame page

9   The border between the two frames can be removed. Return to Normal mode on the index page, then right-click in the left frame and select **Frame Properties** again. Click on the **Frames Pages** button, and on the **Frames** tab set **Frame spacing** to zero and make sure that the **Show Borders** box is not ticked.

10 You can work directly in the side frame. Add links to other pages. Save the pages.

11 Select **File**, then **Preview in Browser**, and check that all the pages load correctly from your navigation bar.

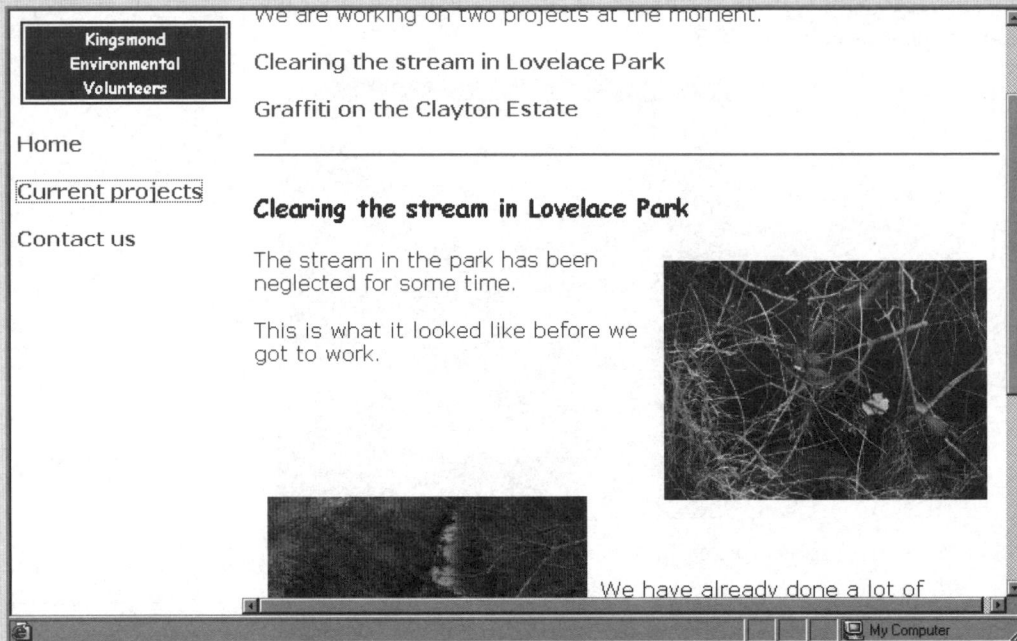

Figure 11.5 The contents of the main frame can scroll past the fixed left frame

Finishing the site

You might like to add an image map, identifying the location of all the projects. Metatags should be added before publishing the site.

→ **Practise your skills 1**

1 Draw a storyboard for a new web. It should use frames. The frame along the top should hold the navigation links.

2 Indicate the length of the frames in pixels.

3 In FrontPage start a new empty web.

4 As before, set up a style sheet and a template.

5 Create the home page, and save it as home.htm (not index.htm).

6 Create the page that contains the navigation links.

7 Set up the frames page, and save it as index.htm

8 Set the initial pages for each frame.

9 Continue to build the web.

→ **Check your knowledge**

1 What is a frame page?

Use graphics software to create and manipulate images for web pages

You will learn to

- Explain the factors that affect the file size of an image:
  - ☐ Number of colours
  - ☐ File compression
  - ☐ Physical pixel dimensions
  - ☐ File type
- Use file compression to achieve optimal quality of images within constraints (file size, download times)
- Apply transparency to images
- Describe the advantage of 'transparency' when applied to an image
- Apply 'web-safe' palettes of colours to images
- Explain the purpose of using a 'web-safe' palette of colours

If you want to prepare images for use on a web page, the best option is to use specialist graphics software. General painting packages, such as Microsoft Paint, can be used to create images and also to manipulate existing images. You can then save the images in jpg or gif format.

Photo manipulation packages, such as Microsoft Photo Editor, Corel Photo House, or Adobe PhotoShop provide a number of tools that help you to optimise the appearance of photos. They can also be used to work with any ready drawn bitmap image.

Features of images

File size of an image

When you download a web page from the Internet, the browser first of all downloads the actual page file. It then downloads all the image files that are used on the page. If there are a lot of images this can take some time, especially on a slow dial-up connection.

Most of the image files that you use in word processing or desktop publishing take a great deal of memory. The size of the image file can vary from a few kilobytes up to several megabytes. For example, photos taken with a digital camera are often between two and four megabytes in size. If you put one of these on a website and tried to download it, you could be waiting for a long time if you are using a slow modem. For this reason, all images on a website are stored in a compressed format which gives much smaller file sizes.

For most pages, try to limit the total memory size of all the images on a page to 60 kilobytes. Larger images can be used if the user is expecting an image-rich site, or if they are warned that the page may take a while to download.

Information

You can find out how big an image file is on a web. Click on the images folder in the folder list.

Right-click on the image file, and select Properties. The Properties dialogue box tells you how big the file is in kilobytes.

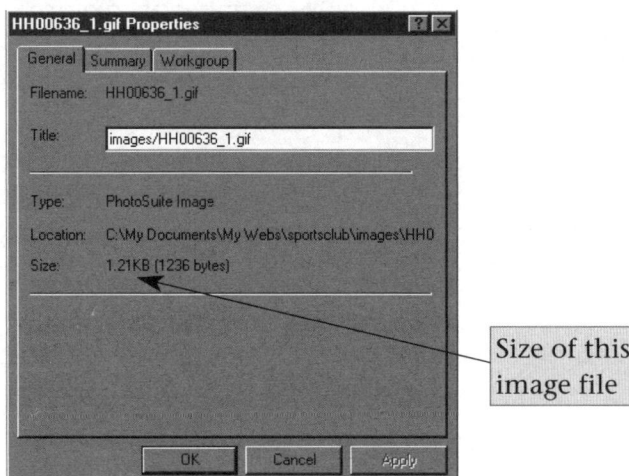

Figure 12.1 The image Properties window

Number of colours

We have already looked at the colour depth of screens. The two image formats that are used on the Internet use differing colour depth.

- jpg – can use 16 or 24 bit colour values.
- gif – only uses 8 bit colour values.

The jpg format usually uses 24 bit colour values. This provides over 16 million different colours, which is more than can be distinguished by the human eye, and is the reason why jpgs are used for photos.

The gif format uses 8 bit colour values which provides only 256 different colours. Gifs are ideal for simple icons and line drawings.

File compression

The package will offer you some choice over the level of compression for jpgs. A more compressed photo will take up less memory, but will also display less detail. If you are asked to choose the **quality** select 75%; on the other hand if you are asked to specify the **degree of compression** select 25%. These two choices have exactly the same effect as each other, but unfortunately software packages are not consistent in the way they ask the question.

Manipulating compressed images

Once an image has been saved in a compressed form, gif or jpg, you should not try to manipulate it any further. If the image is compressed for a second time the quality may suffer noticeably. Always go back to the original version before it was compressed if you want to make any more changes.

You may not have access to the bitmap version of an image and may only have its jpg format, for example, if you use a picture from a photo CD. After you have reduced the size, save the image again as a jpg, but this time choose 100% quality or 0% compression. If you compress the image a second time the image may become distorted. Check the memory used. If it is too large then experiment with a small amount of compression.

Dimensions of an image

Most photos should be cropped before being used on a web page. You need to cut out the unnecessary parts of the picture and just focus on the key elements. Photos on a website do not have to conform to any of the standard picture ratios, and can be any shape. If you need to crop a picture do so before you reduce the dimensions.

Images are usually reduced in size before use on a web page. It is not a good idea to enlarge an existing image. Enlarged images often suffer from the 'jaggies', which is a nickname for the jagged edges that you sometimes see on graphics.

Figure 12.2 A case of the jaggies in an image that has been enlarged

File type

The jpg format uses 3 bytes per pixel and, as such, takes up more memory than the gif format. Also, the method of compression is rather different, and beyond the scope of this unit, but the effect is to make gifs far more economical in terms of memory.

If you do need photorealistic images, or you need to match colours exactly, then you should use the jpg format. Otherwise, experiment with the gif format to see if it produces an acceptable image. Web pages download much more quickly if the images are in gif format.

Transparency

Images saved in gif format can use the transparency property. Graphics software will allow you to identify a colour on the image which is to be made transparent. When the image is then inserted onto a web page the page background is seen through the transparent area. This means that you can create a diagram or cartoon which appears to be part of the page and is not surrounded by a different colour.

Using animated gifs

The gif format can be used to create short, repeating animated sequences. Many examples of these are displayed on websites, and there are many free sources on the Internet. Animated gifs should be used, if at all, with very great care. The eye is drawn to an animation, especially if it lies on the periphery of vision, and can distract the visitor from the main content.

As a general rule, animated gifs should only be used to draw attention directly to an item on the page, such as a warning, or to request that a visitor take action straightaway (e.g. to confirm some information that they have input), or for amusement.

Web-safe colours

Colour codes

24 bit colours, as used for jpgs and bitmaps, are stored in RGB (Red, Green, Blue) format. 8 bits are used for each of the three colours, and combinations of these three primary colours gives all the possible hues. The RGB codes consist of three numbers, each of which has a value from 0 (none of that colour) to 255 (maximum colour).

In a style sheet you will see that colours are expressed like this:

rgb(51, 102, 204)

Thus, rgb(51, 102, 204) has some red, more green and a lot of blue, and displays as a strong mid blue.

Black is the complete absence of colour so has the code rgb(0, 0, 0), while white is created by combining all colours and has the code rgb(255, 255, 255). It can be quite tricky working out colour codes for a particular shade from scratch, but colour charts can be found on the Internet. Colours in graphics packages are determined in a similar way.

The numerical value of a colour can be expressed in decimal (0 to 255) or hexadecimal (#00 to #FF) numbers. Thus, rgb(51, 102, 204) is the same as #3366CC (# is used to denote hexadecimal numbers).

Web-safe colour codes

The appearance of colours does vary from screen to screen, even when set at the same colour depth. A limited number of colours have been found to appear clearly and without dithering on all screens. These are known as the web-safe colours.

In FrontPage you may have noticed that only a limited number of colour values are used in the predesigned style sheets – 0, 51, 102, 153, 204, 255. The hex equivalents are 00, 33, 66, 99, CC, FF. Colours constructed with one of these values for each of the three RGB components make up the web-safe colours, thus rgb(153, 0, 51) is a web-safe colour, whilst rgb(57, 139, 17) is not.

That does not mean that you should never use colours outside the web-safe list – photos normally contain many such colours. But if a colour is to be used over a large area, for example, as a background colour, then you should choose from the web-safe palette.

→ Practise your skills 1

1 If you have access to a painting package (other than Microsoft Paint) or a photo manipulation package (other than Microsoft Photo Editor), then familiarise yourself with its features.

2 See how many of the following you can carry out:
- Use the painting/drawing tools.
- Add text to an image.
- Rotate or flip an image.
- Save an image in gif format.
- Apply transparency to a gif.
- Save an image in jpg format, using appropriate compression.
- Identify the file size of an image.

→ Check your knowledge

1 Why are images on a web page stored in a compressed format?
2 What kinds of images are usually stored in the jpg or gif formats?
3 What are the jaggies and how do you avoid them?
4 What are web-safe colours and why should you use them?

You will learn to

- Verify that all links work as expected
- Use different browsers to preview pages and verify that all components appear as expected

The website goes live at the moment when it is **published**, that is, when it is uploaded to a web server and becomes accessible to visitors. Before that happens the site should be subjected to thorough technical testing. Once the site is published some additional testing must be carried out.

Technical testing

Before a site is published on the Internet, it should be subjected to thorough technical testing, and the tests should all be repeated after the site has been published, along with additional tests. These tests should be constructed to check that the final website matches the original design specification, bearing in mind any amendments that may have been made to the design specification during the prototyping stage.

The technical design of a website concentrates on several usability issues:

- Navigation – should be tested both before and after publishing.
- Use of search tools – best tested after publishing.
- Download times – best tested after publishing.
- Browser compatibility – should be tested both before and after publishing.
- Maintenance – best tested with the client after publishing.

All websites should be fully tested before they go live. They should then be tested again after they have been uploaded to the Internet. Similar tests should also be done whenever a site is updated.

Images

- Check that each image occupies the intended space on the screen and is positioned correctly.
- Select the properties of each image to check how much memory each uses. Do not forget to include any graphical buttons or bullets that you have used. Calculate the total memory used by all the images on each page. Aim to keep the total to under 60 KB per page.
- If you want to use a larger image (for example, if you want to offer your visitor the chance to see a full size photo) you should warn the visitor before they link to the page that it will be a slow download.

Hint:

All testing should be carried out in a browser, not in the Preview mode of a web authoring package. The site can be opened in a browser by navigating to the position of the index page on the local drive.

Layout

- Check that each page appears as intended in your usual browser.
- Check the whole site on an earlier version of the browser you are using.
- Check the whole site on a different browser.

Verify links

Before the site is uploaded the home page should be opened in a browser. Several tests should be carried out:

- Check that each of the links from the main navigation bar loads the correct page.
- Check that the links in the main navigation bar on all other pages behave as expected.
- Check all the internal links on each page.

It is important to document the tests carried out on a site as you do it. It is very easy to lose track of the tests you have done, and then to repeat tests unnecessarily, or even leave some out.

When checking links it is useful to create a table like this:

Page: products.htm

Link to	OK?	Notes
contacts.htm	✓	
home.htm	✓	
cartridges.htm	Bad link	Update this

Preview in different browsers

Web pages do not appear exactly the same in each browser. The variations that can affect the appearance of a page include:

- The screen resolution – usually 800 or 1024 pixels wide.
- The browser used – usually Internet Explorer or Netscape, although there are some other browsers, such as Opera, which are used by smaller numbers of visitors.
- The version of the browser that is used – old versions continue to be used around the world long after much newer versions have been launched.

The site should first be checked in the resident browser at both 800 and 1024 screen resolutions. The full width of each page should be visible at 800 pixels without scrolling sideways. The site should also look reasonable when a full size window is opened at 1024 width.

The site should then be checked in the alternative browser at both resolutions. If possible, the site should then be checked in the oldest versions of each browser that are available.

Changes may have to be made to the pages to ensure that the displays in all cases are as compatible as possible and that any minor differences are acceptable.

Hint:

Both Internet Explorer and Netscape can be downloaded for free from their respective websites.

Testing a website after uploading

Immediately after a site has been uploaded to the web server, it should be tested by entering the URL in a browser.

The full set of technical tests should then be repeated. The most common errors found at this stage occur if a file has not been uploaded, or if one has been uploaded to an incorrect remote directory. Additional technical testing can be carried out. The designer should:

- Test each external link to ensure that it loads the correct site.
- Test how long it takes to download each page, including all the images, using the slowest dial-up connections.

Evaluation against specification

The website will have been reviewed with the client throughout its development, but the finished site must be subjected to a final review with the client against the original specification. At this stage any errors that emerge can be dealt with.

→ **Practise your skills 1**

1 Open the four page web that you completed in Section 10.
2 Use the information from this section to test the web thoroughly before it is uploaded to the server.

→ **Check your knowledge**

1 Why should you check a web page in more than one browser?
2 Why should you check a web page at different screen resolutions?
3 Why should you check all the links within pages and to other pages on the same website?
4 Why should you check web pages again **after** uploading to the server?

Section 14 | Publish and maintain web pages

You will learn to

- Publish (upload) websites to Internet/intranet or other web servers
- Identify how sites can be promoted (register with search engine, advertise, exchange links with other sites)
- State the need for security when sending certain types of information across the Internet

In order to publish a website on the Web you need:

- Access to web space on a web server.
- A domain name that points to the website on the server.
- The means to transfer the pages and other files to the web space.

Web servers and web hosts

Information

- A **web server** is a computer linked to the Internet which stores one or more websites.
- A **web host** is a company that owns one or more web servers, and rents out space on the web servers to others.

All the files and folders that make up a website must be uploaded to a web server before they can be made available on the Internet. A large commercial organisation may own its own web server, but the majority of websites are hosted by web hosts.

Most Internet Service Providers (ISPs) also act as web hosts, and many include a certain amount of web space with their accounts. Typically the space will be from 20 MB to 30 MB in size, and this is more than enough for a quite substantial site. Larger amounts of web space can usually be acquired at additional cost.

Information

There are also some specialist web hosting companies that offer web space. These companies can be found easily by searching on the Web for 'web hosts'. Sometimes free space is offered, but this often carries the condition that the site must display some advertising for the host. It may be acceptable to display advertising of this kind on a personal website, but is not appropriate on a website for a commercial enterprise.

Server side scripts

Some sites can only function properly if they are hosted on servers that also store additional support software (or scripts). In each case, the designer must ensure that the web server does support their needs.

Sites developed in FrontPage often include special functions that make use of additional software, known as **FrontPage Server extensions**, stored on the web server. These are not made available by all web servers; in particular, a number of the major ISPs that include web space in their low cost packages do not support FrontPage extensions.

CGI scripts are used on many web servers. FormMail.pl is a script that is used by many web designers to generate emails from data collected by an online form. The ISP will provide the URL of this script on their server.

Registering a domain name

A domain name, such as thisismydomain.co.uk, must be registered with one of the registration organisations. All domain names ending with .uk are registered with Nominet. There are a number of official registries for .com and other domains. A yearly fee is charged for domain name registration.

Domain names are often registered through ISPs who then carry out the formal registration process on behalf of the organisation or individual. Once the domain name has been registered, the ISP will ensure that the domain name points to the correct web space on their web server.

A **Whois server** can be searched to find out which domain names are currently registered and which are still free. Again, most ISPs provide a Whois search facility.

Information

Choosing a domain name can be a challenging task, as many millions of names have already been registered. There have been some legal moves to protect commercial names from being registered by individuals who have no connection with the companies, because in the past so-called cyber-squatters have tried to charge well-known organisations large sums to transfer registered domain names to them.

Uploading a website to a web server

When a website has been tested it can be uploaded (published) to the chosen web server. If the web server is in-house, that is, owned by the organisation, then the system administrators will provide guidance to users about how to transfer the files to the web server.

If an external web server managed by an ISP is used, then all the files and directories will have to be transferred by the designer. This can be done either using the publishing tool built into a web authoring package, or by using File Transfer Protocol (FTP) software. In both cases the following data is needed:

- The domain name.
- The user's name (as registered with the ISP).
- The user's password.

FTP shareware software, free for educational use, can be downloaded from the Internet. To use it the user must be online. A dialogue box asks for the required data, then locates the web space on the remote server. Figure 14.1 shows a typical layout – the left side shows the files and directories on the home computer (local system) and the right side shows the files and directories on the web server (remote system). The user highlights the files and directories to be uploaded from the left side, then clicks on the right pointing arrow to transfer them across.

All the files that make up the site must be transferred, including page files, style sheets, any script files, the images directory and its contents, plus any folders and files that may have been created by the web authoring package.

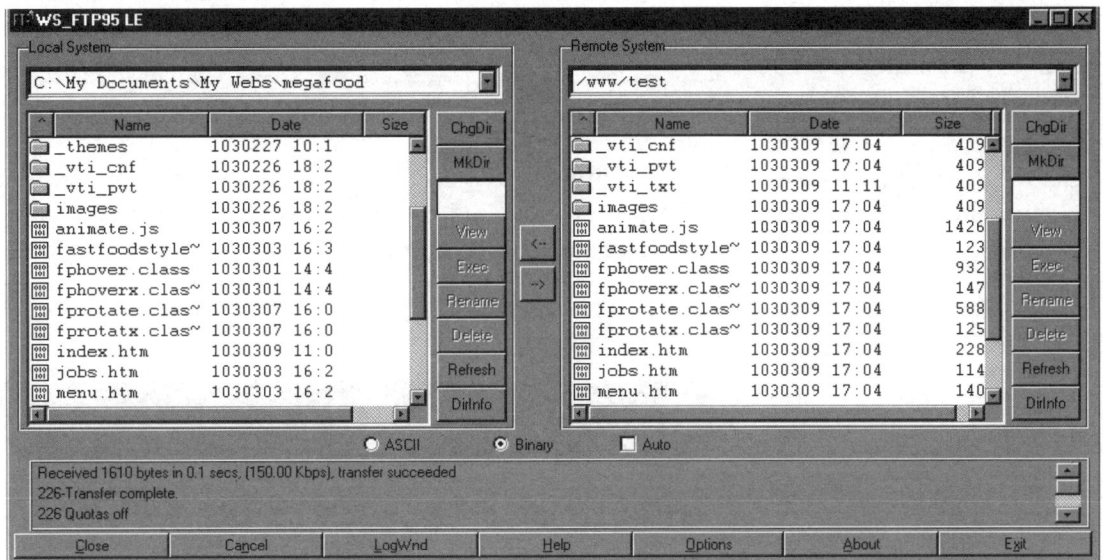

Figure 14.1 FTP software (Ipswitch)

Task 14.1   Publishing a site in FrontPage

Method

1 Open the web that you want to publish.
2 Select **Publish Web** in the **File** menu.
3 Enter the URL of the domain, then click on OK (Figure 14.2).
4 You will then be asked for your username and password, as used with your ISP.
5 In the **Publish Web** dialogue box, click on **Options**, and select **All pages**.
6 An animation records progress, and when the site has been successfully uploaded you will be informed and prompted to view it in your browser.

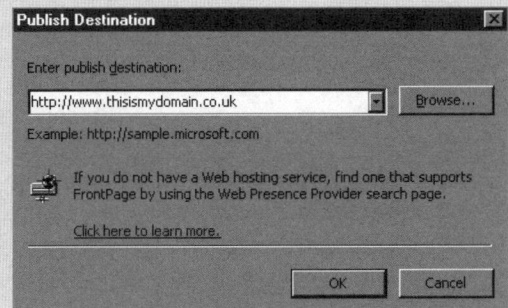

Figure 14.2 The Publish Web dialogue box in FrontPage

Promote a website

Registering a website with search engines

Search engines are continually crawling through the Web by following all the links from one site to another. As they do this, they maintain huge indexing databases about the sites. In particular, they note the keywords and descriptions in the metatags, and they also extract keywords from the text on pages. The indexes are then referred to whenever a user enters text in a search engine.

It can take some time for a search engine to find a new website, but sites can be registered directly with them. Many search engines have UK versions which enable the visitor to restrict the search to UK sites if they wish.

Weblinks:

To access the website content relevant to this page visit www.heinemann. co.uk/hotlinks

Enter express code 2563P, click GO and then click on the relevant link from the text.

Information

The most widely used search engines are Google, AllTheWeb, Yahoo! which is powered by Google, MSN Search and Ask Jeeves. Links to all these sites are given on the Heinemann hotlinks web page.

Internet security

Unauthorised access to the web server

In order to upload files to a web server you only need three items of data – the domain name, plus the username and password for the account.

If a web server is owned by an organisation and connected to its internal network, then unauthorised access may be possible from within the organisation. Employees who have legitimate access to the server can at times be careless with their user IDs. Even if confidentiality is not breached, usernames usually follow a standard pattern within an organisation, and passwords can be guessed. It can sometimes be easy for an employee who wants to damage the organisation, or who simply wants to play a joke, to gain access to the web space and then change the content. Of course, such behaviour would be traceable and would lead to instant dismissal.

Web servers located within organisations can be protected from external interference by firewalls. A web server owned by an ISP is much more vulnerable. Someone who knows the username and password for a domain can gain access to the web space from any computer that is connected to the Internet anywhere in the world.

Secure servers

A web server may hold database files, containing information collected from the website through an online form. Organisations that collect personal data from customers in this way have to be particularly vigilant in protecting their web servers from unauthorised access. They need to do this:

- To comply with the Data Protection Act, 1998.
- To reassure customers that personal data about them will be secure.
- To encourage customers to provide credit card details for online transactions.

A **secure server** encrypts all the data stored on it, so if anyone does gain illegal access they will not be able to understand or use the data. Secure servers are used for all financial transactions over the Internet, and increasingly for the collection of other personal data (see Figure 14.3)

Information

Data is encrypted when it is converted into a secret code. Encrypted data is decrypted when it is converted back to ordinary text.

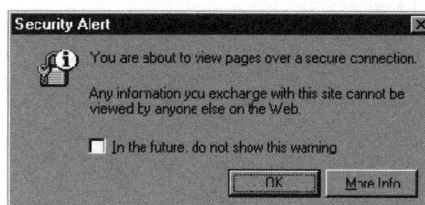

Figure 14.3 Message given when using a secure server

When a website is on a secure server you will see a small padlock icon at the bottom of the window.

Figure 14.4 Indication that site is on a secure server

→ **Practise your skills 1**

1 Using the FrontPage feature, publish your website to a web server. This could be on the Internet or on a local intranet. You may have to obtain advice from the system administrator about the location where it should be published.

2 If you are working on a home computer, check whether your account with your ISP includes web space. If it does, then the instructions you have received from your ISP should tell you the location (URL) of your web space.

→ **Check your knowledge**

1 What are a web server and a web host?

2 What are server side scripts?

3 What is a domain name?

4 Describe two methods for uploading a website to the web server.

5 What is the Computer Misuse Act?

6 Why do some websites use a secure server?

Practice assignments

This section gives you the instructions for carrying out two practice assignments. Each is introduced with a brief scenario which specifies the content of a four page website.

The instructions for carrying out the assignments are stated after the scenarios. You should carry out both Task A and Task B for each scenario.

Scenario 1

You work for a car showroom called The Car Gallery. You have been asked to design a website to advertise new cars for sale.

Cars are categorised as small, family or large. The home page should have links to three further pages, each listing the cars for sale in one of the categories.

Scenario 2

You work in the IT department of SafeInsure, an insurance company. As an employee of the company you have been asked to design a website that gives information about insurance policies.

The website should provide information about three categories of insurance: holiday, car and home insurance.

Instructions

The website will consist of four pages.
- A home page that must contain metatags, links to the three other pages, an email link for enquiries and an external link to another website.
- Three further web pages to hold the information in each of the three categories. Each of these pages will contain details (in a table) of the goods or services in the relevant category, at least one image and a hyperlink to return to the home page
- Every page must have a background image, your name, and the date the page was last updated at the bottom of the page, and the company name and logo at the top of the page.

Task A

In this task you are required to produce a design specification for a website.
1 Create a sketch of the home page to show:
- Company name.
- Company logo.
- EITHER an image map for the three categories to link to appropriate category web pages OR three hyperlinks to link to appropriate category web pages.
- Email link for enquiries.
- One external hyperlink to another website.
- Your name and date last updated.
- EITHER a hyperlink at the bottom of the page to return to the top of the page OR a hyperlink at the top of the page to link to a bookmark.
- Notes to specify font type, font style, font size, font colour.
- Notes to specify background image and metatags.

2 Create a sketch for the three category pages to show:
- Company name.
- Company logo.
- Hyperlink to return to home page.
- Table to hold the details of the goods or services.
- Text.
- One graphical image.
- Your name and date last updated.
- Notes to specify font type, font style, font size, font colour and background image.

3 Draw a structure diagram to show the links between each page of the website.

4 Produce a project plan for the incremental production of the website.

Note that in the assignment that will be assessed, you will be told to hand in the documentation for marking before proceeding to Task B.

Task B

In this task you are required to create and test the website you designed.

1 Create a background effect to be used on all the web pages:
- In a graphics editing package, load in the image that you have selected to use as the background.
- Manipulate the properties of the image so it is suitable for this purpose.
- Save it in an appropriate file format.
- Open a blank HTML page and use the image to set up the background.
- Test that the background will not make text difficult to read and modify the graphics as necessary.

2 Access a library of images: i.e. clip art or Internet, to select the images for inclusion on the web pages. Resize and apply transparency to the images to suit your design and save the images in a suitable format for use on the web pages. Apply file compression where appropriate.

3 Set up the home page as specified in your design.

4 Create a template for the three category web pages as specified in your design.

5 Use the template to create the three category web pages.

6 Ensure that appropriate alignment attributes have been set for the graphical images.

7 Add additional information for the graphical images using the image Alt attribute to notify users that an image exists if it cannot be displayed in their browser.

8 Check that all links work as specified in the design.

9 Preview the web pages in two different browsers and check that all components appear as expected.

10 Upload the website to a web server.

11 Check that all links work, as specified in the design, on the web server.

12 Check that all components appear as expected on the web server.

13 Print out the HTML code for all the web pages.

Solutions

Section 1 Check your knowledge

1 Screen resolution is the number of pixels that are displayed on the screen. The most common resolutions are 1280 × 960, 1024 × 768 and 800 × 600.

2 Many users find horizontal scrollbars irritating, and do not scroll to the right to see the full width of a page when it does not fit into the browser window.

3 Colour depth is the number of colours that form the 'palette' from which colours can be selected to be displayed on a screen. Options include 32 bit (millions of colours), 16 bit (65,536 different colours), 8 bit (256 colours) and 4 bit (the 16 standard colours).

4 The usability of a site is the extent to which it is easy to use by a normal user. You should check how readable the text is (font, size, colours, style of language) and how the user can navigate around the site.

5 A browser uses the URL to send a request to the web server. It then downloads the page which will normally be in HTML code. It then interprets the code and displays the page. It continues to download all the files, such as images, that are also used on the page.

6 gif and jpg.

Section 2 Check your knowledge

1 Web authoring software allows you to design web pages without needing to know how to write HTML code. You can lay out the pages in the WYSIWYG editor and the software generates the HTML code for you. You can also use the software to view and amend the code created.

2 A tag is a formatting instruction. In HTML tags are surrounded by angled brackets, like this: <p>

3 The definition of the font, size, colour etc. is added to every paragraph that is formatted.

4 If you have used the styles from the style list, then a design theme creates a consistent look to all your pages.

5 You can define your own styles (font, colour, size, borders, shading etc.) for each of the styles in the style list.

Section 3 Check your knowledge

1 You can upload a photo from a digital camera, you can scan in a normal printed photo, or you can find sources of copyright free photos on the Web.

2 Photos can be manipulated in photo editing software. They can be changed in size, and then saved in jpg format. (Note that photo editing packages offer many other functions as well.)

3 You can change, for the selected image, the alignment, the horizontal and vertical spacing, the thickness of the border etc.

4 To display data in a tabular form, and to layout the contents of a page.

Section 4 Check your knowledge

1 This is an approach to web design which involves the client (or end user) throughout the design process. Prototypes are used to demonstrate the appearance of a website at an early stage so that modifications can be made before it has been fully implemented.

2 User requirements analysis, prototyping and implementation, technical testing and publishing, evaluation.

3 E-commerce uses a website to sell goods or services.

4 By age, sex, interests, location or activities.

5 A set of web pages which are viewable by anyone within an organisation, but not over the Internet.

Section 5 Check your knowledge

1 Basic information about the organisation, contact details, privacy policy (if data is collected from visitors).

2 A set of sketches to show the appearance of each of the pages on a website. Notes should also indicate the function of any buttons and other links.

3 In a formal top-down linking structure, a page that has links to pages below it in the structure is known as the parent page. The pages it links to are its child pages.

4 A set of navigation buttons arranged in a row along the top of a page or as a column down the side.

5 The browser window can display two or more frames, each of which holds the contents of a single webpage. The contents of one can change independently of the other.

Section 6 Check your knowledge

1 The first page that is downloaded from the web server. It is often the home page, but it could contain the instructions for setting up the frames for the site.
2 Email links, and downloads. (Also links to bookmarks on the same page.)
3 Items of data held in the head of the HTML code. Search engines use metatags to identify what a web page is about.

Section 7 Check your knowledge

1 A page that can be used over and over again as the basis for other pages.
2 An embedded style sheet is stored on the page that it applies to, and it only affects that page. An external style sheet is a separate file; any number of pages can refer to it, so it can be applied to all the pages on a website.

Section 8 Check your knowledge

1 It holds some text that is displayed in place of the image if the user decides not to download any images. This is particularly important for blind users.
2 A small version of an image, which is then used as a link to a page containing the full sized image.

Section 9 Check your knowledge

1 Cell spacing is the space (measured in pixels) between one cell and the next. Cell padding is the space between the side or top of each cell and the contents.
2 A table can fix the images and text on the page, so that they do not move when size of the window is changed. This enables the designer to specify the exact position of items on the screen.
3 A position on the page that is identified and named in the HTML code. A hyperlink elsewhere on the page can link directly to the bookmark.

Section 11 Check your knowledge

1 The code on a frame page defines the size and position of the frames. It also identifies the web pages that will sit in each frame.

Section 12 Check your knowledge

1 Images have to be downloaded from a web server and the transfer times on a modem link can be quite slow. Images, especially photos, can take up a large amount of memory, but when they are compressed they can transfer rapidly.
2 The jpg format is normally used for photos and the gif format for simple line drawings.
3 Jagged images caused by enlarging a bitmap or jpg image. These should never be enlarged.
4 Web-safe colours appear without dithering on any screen, no matter what colour depth or screen resolution has been set. Only web-safe colours should be used for large areas of colour, such as backgrounds.

Section 13 Check your knowledge

1 Browsers interpret the HTML code in slightly different ways. Sometimes a page does not look the same in different browsers.
2 To ensure that the page appears satisfactorily for all visitors. If the page is resizable then it should resize appropriately. If it is fixed size then it should look sensible at all resolutions.
3 Because errors can easily be made.
4 To ensure that all the files have been uploaded successfully, and to check that links to other websites work properly.

Section 14 Check your knowledge

1 A web server is a computer that holds one or more websites and is linked directly to the Internet. A web host is a company that owns a web server and rents out webspace.
2 Software that is held on the web server and can be used by web pages. FrontPage Extensions are server side scripts that are needed in order to run some of the functions offered in FrontPage.
3 A domain name is a name that is registered officially and can then be used to identify websites and for email addresses.
4 In FrontPage a website can be uploaded to the server by using the publishing function in the software. Alternatively, FTP software can be used.
5 The Computer Misuse Act makes any unauthorised access to a computer system illegal.
6 The data held on a secure server is encrypted. It is used to store sensitive personal data, such as credit card numbers on e-commerce sites.

Outcomes matching guide

	Outcome 1 Describe and apply the basics of web page development	
	Practical activities	
1	Achieve desired effects for: • Pages (set suitable default background page and text colours, background image) • Text (font, size, style and colour) • Paragraphs (paragraph and line breaks, indentation) a) Using text editor to apply HTML tags b) WYSIWYG HTML editing tools	Section 2
2	Convert images into formats suitable for inclusion on web pages	Sections 3, 8, 12
	Underpinning knowledge	
1	Describe the effects that different screen resolutions and colour depths have on web pages	Section 1
2	Explain the significance of the speed of the Internet connection between the user's computer and the Internet (different file sizes and download times)	Section 1
3	Describe the main features and capabilities found in web browsers	Section 1
4	State the main features of the Hypertext Markup Language (HTML) and identify its limitations	Sections 1, 2
5	Describe the importance of the pixel	Section 1
6	Explain the advantages and disadvantages between different graphics file formats suitable for use in a web page	Sections 1, 12
7	Explain the issues involving copyright relevant to Internet websites	Section 1
	Outcome 2 Undertake user requirements analysis	
	Practical activities	
1	Design websites for target audience using storyboarding	Section 5
2	Create appropriate structure diagrams demonstrating the linking structure of web pages	Section 5
3	Produce project plans for the incremental development of websites, including the gathering of suitable resources	Section 5
	Underpinning knowledge	
1	Identify the functions of different websites, for example: educational, governmental, and commercial (reference, selling, promotion, entertainment)	Section 4
2	Describe the term 'target audience'	Section 4
3	Identify the importance of 'house style'	Section 5
4	Explain the relative merits of different page layout styles (standard, tables and frames)	Sections 5, 9, 11
5	Identify how maintenance and further development need to be considered during design	Section 4
	Outcome 3 Use appropriate development tools to implement web pages	
	Practical activities	
1	Create templates for pages used within a website based upon house styles	Sections 7, 10
2	Embed images within web pages: a) Set suitable alignment attributes b) Use the Alt tag to provide the user with alternative meaningful information	Sections 3, 8
3	Use tables to enhance layout of: a) Text and graphics b) Tabular information	Sections 3, 9
4	Use anchors (bookmarks) to establish hyperlinks within a single web page	Section 9
5	Use hyperlinks to link to: a) Pages within the same website b) Other sites on the World Wide Web c) Email d) FTP	Section 6
6	Create image maps	Section 6
7	Use metatags to add keyword information to pages to aid search engines	Section 6

Outcome 4 Test websites	
Practical activities	
1	Verify all links work as expected	Section 13
2	Use different browsers to preview pages and verify all components appear as expected	Section 13

Outcome 5 Use graphics software to create and manipulate images on a web page	
Practical activities	
1	Resize images within websites: a) For use as background images on pages b) For use as icons or thumbnails c) To specific dimensions	Section 8
2	Apply transparency to images	Section 8
3	Use file compression to achieve optimal quality of images within constraints (file size, download times)	Section 12
4	Apply 'web-safe' palettes of colours to images	Section 12
Underpinning knowledge	
1	Explain the factors that affect the file size of an image: a) Number of colours b) File compression c) Physical pixel dimensions d) File type	Section 12
2	Describe the advantage of 'transparency' when applied to an image	Section 8
3	Explain the purpose of using a 'web-safe' palette of colours	Section 12

Outcome 6 Publish and maintain websites	
Practical activities	
1	Use software to manage the development of websites	Sections 6, 14
2	Publish (upload) websites to Internet/intranet or other web servers	Section 14
Underpinning knowledge	
1	Identify how site can be promoted (register with search engine, advertise, exchange links with other sites)	Section 14
2	State the need for security when sending certain types of information across the Internet	Section 14